Lawton Fort Sill

The Lawton Fort Sill Chamber of Commerce is pleased to sponsor
Silent Witness: The Diary of a Historic Tree at Fort Sill by Towana Spivey.

This book provides a fascinating look into the history of Fort Sill.

We invite you to enjoy the book today and for years to come.

On the cover: The Silent Witness bur oak tree posing with the author in the forests along Medicine Bluffs Creek. Insets of General William T. Sherman and the Kiowa War Chief Se-tain'te (Satanta). (Photographer: Jetawn Spivey) (AUTH)

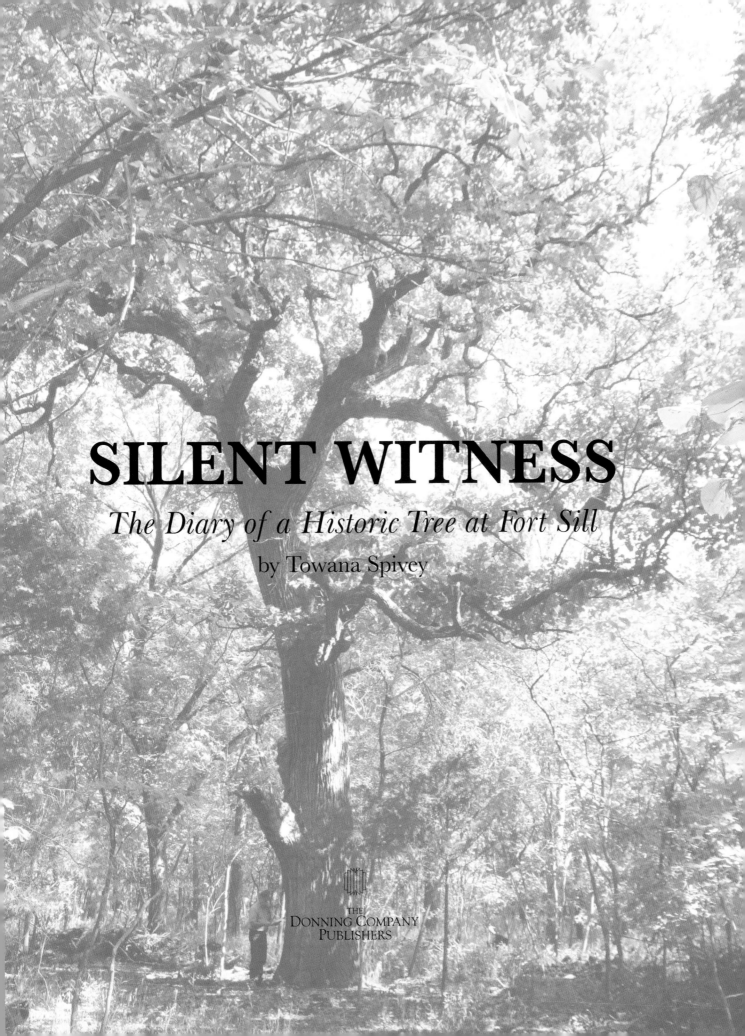

SILENT WITNESS

The Diary of a Historic Tree at Fort Sill

by Towana Spivey

THE
DONNING COMPANY
PUBLISHERS

The Donning Company Publishers
184 Business Park Drive, Suite 206
Virginia Beach, VA 23462

Steve Mull, General Manager
Barbara Buchanan, Office Manager
Wendy Nelson and Pamela Koch, Editors
Brett Oliver, Graphic Designer
Derek Eley, Imaging Artist
Jeanie Akins, Project Research Coordinator
Tonya Hannink, Marketing Specialist
Pamela Engelhard, Marketing Advisor

Ed Williams, Project Director

Library of Congress Cataloging-in-Publication Data

Spivey, Towana.
  Silent witness : the diary of a historic tree at Fort Sill / By Towana Spivey.
    p. cm.
  Includes bibliographical references.
  ISBN 978-1-57864-639-5 (hard cover : alk. paper)
  1. Fort Sill (Okla.)—History. 2. Fort Sill (Okla.)—Biography. 3. Historic trees—Oklahoma—Fort Sill. 4. Indians of North America—Oklahoma—Fort Sill Region—History. I. Title.
  F704.F74S65 2010
  976.6'48--dc22
                                2010023726

Printed in the United States of America at Walsworth Publishing Company

Table of Contents

Acorns and leaves from the Silent Witness bur oak tree. (Photographer: Jetawn Spivey) (AUTH)

Illustrations

Photo Credits: (NA) National Archives; (SI) Smithsonian Institution; (FSM) Fort Sill Museum; (OHS) Oklahoma Historical Society; (MGP) Museum of the Great Plains; (45th IDM) 45th Infantry Division Museum; (DA) Department of Army; (RM) Robert G. McCubbin; (GH) Gary Hendershott; (AUTH) Author.

Foreword

History is generally viewed and studied only by those who have fascination for the past. Unfortunately, those who study the past are but a small percentage of the American population. It is unfortunate because the past is deeply connected with the present, and knowing the fortunes and misfortunes of life, one then has the capacity to improve the living of life today and tomorrow. The only element that keeps that possibility intact is the dedication of men and women who continue to keep the past alive in the form of writing.

Towana Spivey, a member of the Chickasaw Nation and a passionate historian, has for almost thirty years directed the Fort Sill National Historic Landmark Museum, one of the richest historical settings in our country. Not only has he protected and preserved this marvelous place, but through fervent dedication, he has managed to develop it as well.

His latest book shares the remarkable multitude of intriguing events that have taken place in southwestern Oklahoma. *Silent Witness* provides knowledge of everything from the sacred earth in the area (Medicine Bluffs), to the Native Americans (Comanche, Kiowa, and Apache), the military (Custer, Sherman, Sheridan, etc.), prominent civilians, and many other telling elements.

What makes *Silent Witness* so unique is that these revealing stories come from a stellar being living on this earth for approximately 250 years, a gigantic bur oak tree, recounting everything that has happened during its presence.

Towana Spivey's connection with this bur oak tree not only gives the reader an unconventionally accurate look at the past, it provides both images and words that emerge directly from the heart and soul of life on earth.

— MICHAEL BLAKE

To "Grandma Lynn"—
who made it possible for me to learn from the past.

Acknowledgments

This unique journey would not have been possible without the support and encouragement of numerous people. Particularly noteworthy is my family, who were always patient and willing to listen as I struggled through the many versions of this project. My wife Phyllis and daughter Mariah often endured the endless, one-sided discussions with myself and always responded with encouragement to move ahead. My son Jetawn and his wife Monica provided valuable assistance with the images and also important technical advice regarding the complicated digital world to this technologically challenged time traveler from the past.

Appreciation is also due to my longtime friend Michael Blake, award-winning author and screenplay writer of *Dances with Wolves* as well as other notable works. He found merit in the project and graced my efforts with his encouragement, resulting in the Foreword for this book.

I am likewise indebted to the pitifully small staff of the Fort Sill National Historic Landmark Museum for their tireless efforts and support in preserving the history while continually being confronted with the many challenges endemic to the army. Mention should be made of the countless and anonymous visitors to the museum whose continuing expressions of interest and thirst for knowledge reflected their keen sense of appreciation for the history of Fort Sill. Acknowledgment is also due the post commander and his wife, MG and Mrs. David Halverson, who were a catalyst for change in preserving the cultural heritage of Fort Sill.

I would be particularly remiss if I did not acknowledge the ultimate inspiration for this project, the ancient oak tree that has relentlessly maintained its vigil on Medicine Bluffs Creek for lo these many years. It has miraculously survived the ravages of time and witnessed the unique history of Fort Sill for many generations.

—THE AUTHOR

Presumptuous man! The reason wouldst thou find,
why form'd so weak, so little, and so blind?

First, if thou canst, the harder reason guess,
why form'd no weaker, blinder, and no less?

Ask of thy mother earth, why oaks were made,
taller or weaker than the weeds they shade?

From *An Essay on Man*
by Alexander Pope
(1688–1744)

Introduction

The following narrative reflects a summary history of Fort Sill, Oklahoma, and its larger context, as told from the perspective of a bur oak tree, *Quercus macrocarpa Michaux*, also referred to as Mossycup Oak. I first became aware of this magnificent tree during the mid-1970s as part of a study I was conducting on historic trees in Oklahoma.

The setting for this giant tree consists of a small forested area discreetly hidden along the banks of the Medicine Bluffs Creek within the Fort Sill Military Reservation. The forested enclave surrounding the oak tree is immediately adjacent to a heavily used golf course. A striking paradox in time is indicated by the fact that this large tree has escaped death and destruction for such a long time while in the immediate proximity of a military training and public recreational area. The fact that it was hidden in plain sight is probably the reason for its survival.

As an employee of the U.S. Forest Service in my early years, and as an archeologist and historian later in my career, I have often encountered large trees of different species tucked away out of sight in remote places. Some were obviously around during the pre-settlement days and, for one reason or another, had survived the many hazards that often accompany the virtues of progress.

Unfortunately, I have also witnessed the unnecessary loss of many historic trees due to a thoughtless disregard for the history and a misguided or exaggerated justification that the trees were standing in the way of progress. It is even worse when that catch-all justification of "safety" is used to remove a historic tree, leaving little defense for anyone trying to save the tree. Without a doubt, this lack of understanding and sensitivity has resulted in major losses to our own

Full view of the bur oak tree on Medicine Bluffs Creek with the author in October 2008 (Photographer: Jetawn Spivey) (AUTH)

Vertical view of deeply incised bark and large nodule on the Silent Witness tree that are typically found on the trunk of an older bur oak tree (Photographer: Jetawn Spivey) (AUTH)

century blacksmith shop and trading post associated with the early history of Fort Sill lay directly in the path of the construction and would have to be removed.

It seemed so obviously unnecessary, and after consulting with the colonel who was in charge of the project for the Tulsa District Army Corps of Engineers, he readily agreed to deviate from the proposed path in order to spare the trees. Our discussions soon revealed that his conservation values originated in his youth when he was an Eagle Scout, and upon reaching maturity, he had continued working with the Boy Scouts as an adult leader. I was very impressed with both his attitude and his flexibility in this matter. Conversely, in the fall of 2008, I was unsuccessful in saving one of the few remaining historic hackberry trees that were planted on the Post Quadrangle in 1875 by the famous frontier Indian fighter and Fort Sill commander, Colonel Ranald S. Mackenzie.

Experiences such as this prompted me to gather as much data as possible about the bur oak tree located on Medicine Bluffs Creek and its relationship with the history of Fort Sill before it, too, faced an uncertain future. As a standard procedure, I measured the circumference around the main trunk at four feet above ground level and also recorded measurements of one of the larger primary or horizontal limbs at its base. Certain of these lower branches were so massive in circumference that they rivaled the trunks of most trees one might commonly encounter elsewhere. Due to the many other surrounding trees at the time, it was very difficult to determine the total horizontal spread of the crown and the actual height of the tree itself.

Over the years I formed a rather unusual relationship with this giant tree, and I would frequently check on it after each major lightning or windstorm to confirm or assess any damages. The constant threat of it being removed by government contractors or others for some inconceivable purpose was another reason to visit regularly. My routine visits became analogous to checking on a grandparent or elderly friend that was unable to get out of the house very often.

history when viable alternatives were available. Regrets and afterthoughts are of little value once the deed has been done.

The inevitable happened in 1974–1975 while I was conducting an archeological survey along the proposed path for a buried municipal water supply line extending from Waurika Lake in Jefferson County to Lake Ellsworth in Comanche County, Oklahoma. Along the southeast boundary of the Fort Sill Military Reservation, the route of the pipeline cut through a narrow belt of virgin timber lining an ancient tributary of East Cache Creek. Several very large trees adjacent to a nineteenth-

On one occasion after a spring windstorm in 1995, I discovered that one of the largest limbs had fallen and was sprawled across the leaf-strewn ground beneath the tree for some distance to the northeast of the trunk. It was not a mortal wound, but one that certainly reduced the total volume of the tree in a noticeable way. To a human being this would have been the equivalent of losing an arm or a leg, and I could almost feel a sympathetic pain for the tree.

The trunk and lower limbs exhibit numerous large, nodule bumps or burls on the surface that normally indicate concentrated cellular or cancerous-like growth patterns on older trees. These burls are highly sought after by woodworkers for special projects, since they are characterized by very tight, swirling grain patterns. Historically, many of the local tribes of the area, such as the Kiowa and Comanche, often removed these burls to create wooden bowls for pounding meat, berries, and other foodstuffs.

As my personal relationship with this monarch of the forest developed over the years, I began to look at the tree as a survivor and a witness to all that had occurred around it over a long period of time. The tree had seen a lot of history and had lived to tell about it. The only element missing was the voice of an "interpreter." Someone was needed to translate the memories experienced by the tree in order to fulfill its destiny. The comparison of the tree as a survivor and witness to history with my own circumstances as the director and curator of the Fort Sill National Historic Landmark Museum for many years was unavoidable.

This task proved to be more complicated than anticipated. First, the interpreter had to be knowledgeable about the history of Fort Sill, including the many incidents and the groups of people who came and went over time. Secondly, the interpreter had to assume the persona of the tree itself in order to properly represent the perspective of the tree.

Learning to think and reason from the perspective of a tree was not taught in any schools I attended while growing up. The tendency to oversimplify and write from an adolescent point of view was difficult to avoid at times. It was also important to portray how the tree reacted to unfamiliar activities and to characterize them accordingly. While the perspective of the tree may sometimes appear naïve in understanding all that it has witnessed, it also reflects the cumulative experience and knowledge of an elder or senior citizen.

To preserve the unique perspective of the tree in recounting history, I decided to forego the practice of using footnotes in the text. While this may present some problems for certain readers, it was deemed necessary in this case. Although reference is occasionally made to specific details or obscure historical facts, in general I tried to avoid such details as the exact month or day of the year when an event occurred. From the perspective of the tree, the event happened during a seasonal cycle or in broad reference to other related incidents.

Since the tree was not part of a prejudicial or politically correct world that either utilized or otherwise strived to avoid negative references and treatment, it saw the various ethnic groups that were active in the area from a perspective based on their obvious differences, such as personal appearance or the chronology of their presence. The Anglo or Euro-American groups were simply described as "light-colored people," while the African American soldiers were referred to as "dark-colored people." The term "native people" was used to distinguish the indigenous populations in the area from those who came later.

An additional consideration was to develop some means of communication between the tree and the distant world that was out of its sight. The "grapevine" that was so interconnected with other trees throughout the forest and across the landscape provided one solution to this problem. It served as the telephone or telegraph across the forest that bordered the major streams and their tributaries throughout the region. Likewise, migratory birds, squirrels, and other animals were capable of carrying the news of the day from tree to tree across greater distances.

Many of the younger oak trees in the immediate vicinity actually originated from acorns that had naturally fallen from the primary oak to the forest floor, or had been distributed by the birds and animals of the forest. In addition to the later generation of oak trees, there were also redbud, elm, hackberry, and assorted other species nearby that formed the nucleus of a family—the children, grandchildren, and friends who gathered around the monarch to provide safety and security for the senior family member. This support group protected the giant oak tree from the high winds and helped keep it out of sight when danger lurked nearby. In keeping with the standard tenets of anthropology, I began to recognize cultural attributes and associations among the trees and animals of the forest.

In the final analysis, however, it is what it is, an old tree that has survived the ravages of time and the threats of modern civilization. The ability to understand and perhaps empathize with the tree's proximity to history is subject to the reader's imagination, of course. The willingness to recognize and appreciate one's own relationships and experiences within the context of the world around us should naturally follow. Perhaps there is some merit in people learning to "witness" their own individual world from the perspective of a tree.

Signed,
TOWANA SPIVEY
THE INTERPRETER

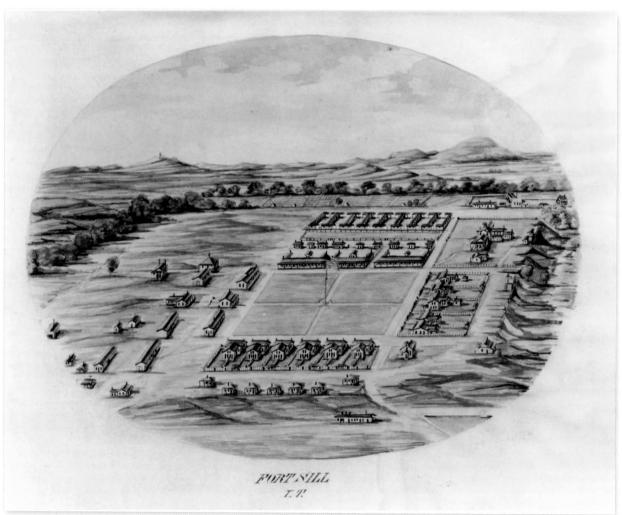

Bird's-eye view, watercolor painting of Fort Sill, Indian Territory, as viewed to the west in 1876. Most of these buildings remain today as part of the Fort Sill National Historic Landmark. (Artist: Unknown Fourth Cavalry soldier) (FSM)

The Diary: A Time of Innocence

It was sometime in the mid-eighteenth century that I sprouted along the banks of Medicine Bluffs Creek near the southeast edge of the Wichita Mountains, and I have witnessed a lot of history in this area since that time. I have experienced many changes in the landscape, the people, and the animals for a long time, and I

have survived to tell about them. A few years after my sprouting, another significant event occurred somewhere far to the east. A new nation that came to be referred to as the United States of America was also born. Little did I realize in those days that the history of this nation would so closely parallel my own and that the decades would so quickly transform into centuries.

I was told by the "Old Ones" of a very ancient tar pit located a few miles to the east of me. It is thought to be over three hundred million years old, and I know it, too, has witnessed a lot of history. Both the animals and the native

View to the west of the natural tar pit on the East Range of Fort Sill. It was originally frequented by pre-dinosaur creatures during the Permian Age approximately three hundred million years ago. In 1852, Captain Randolph Marcy recorded Comanche warriors using the sticky tar from this site on their horses for medicinal purposes. (Photographer: Jetawn Spivey) (AUTH)

Regional map of the southern plains and of the Fort Sill area where much of the history occurred that was reported by the Silent Witness tree (AUTH)

people normally tried to avoid the black, sticky substance oozing from the ground around the fresh water springs. However, there is a subtle but enticing beauty in this picturesque setting, and the native people often came to this place in the past to collect the foul-smelling paste for medicinal purposes. It apparently had a healing

During warm weather, the natural asphalt drains from the main pool through a cut toward the south. The flowing tar continues to capture birds, reptiles, rodents, and insects that will become the fossils of the future. (Photographer: Jetawn Spivey) (AUTH)

effect when the paste was applied as a salve to the wounds or sores on their bodies as well as on their horses.

It also worked well as an adhesive to hold the arrow and spear points on the wooden shafts used for hunting and for war. The natives used the soft red and yellow paint rocks found near the outcroppings of this black sticky substance to decorate themselves and their possessions. It has been my experience that paint rock sources were often regarded as very special, even sacred, to these native people.

To the west I can easily see the magnificent Medicine Bluffs that heaved upward about this same time to a height of 320 feet above the surrounding landscape. These steep, ancient cliffs relentlessly stand guard over the flowing creek at their base and present an imposing break in the landscape between the grassy meadows to the south and the rugged, boulder-strewn mountains to the north. The native people and many varieties of animals have been coming to this region for more generations than I can count to take advantage of the cool, sweet water and the many grassy plants that dominate this area.

Long before my time, the native people routinely hunted the huge mammoth elephants and the giant bison among the grasslands within sight of these high bluffs. Later, the fossil bones of these large animals were occasionally exposed in the deep gullies after the heavy rains washed over their slopes. In more recent times, some of the native people have retrieved the large bones of these extinct creatures and ground them into powder for use in medicines.

The bluffs themselves are regarded as a healing site, and on occasion, I have observed the sacred ceremonies conducted by the native people at the highest point of the cliffs to heal those who were suffering from severe illness. I have also witnessed death on these high bluffs when some of the unfortunate people were not healed and instead died during the ceremonies. Their remains were

View toward the east of the 320-foot-high Medicine Bluffs near Fort Sill, Oklahoma. This site has long been known as a healing place for the tribes in the southern plains. (Photographer: Edward Bates) (FSM)

left to the elements or were buried at various locations along the creek and on the open plains to the south.

Some of the later people who camped along the nearby creek were known as the "Wia-chitoh" or Wichita. These people were farmers and hunters who lived in dome-shaped grass houses near cultivated fields where they raised corn and pumpkins. Another group of native people called the "Numunuh" (the people) or Comanche came into this area when I was but a sapling. They were followed by the "Kai-gwa" or Kiowa and some "Apachu" or Plains Apache a little before 1800, I think. These people lived in conical-shaped tents known as tipis and spent much of their time hunting the buffalo and making war. They also camped around this area and often held their healing ceremonies at the Medicine Bluffs. It has been rumored that some strange people known as the French and the Spanish also

Typical Wichita grass house as seen in the southwest Oklahoma area from the eighteenth into the early twentieth century (Photographer: Edward Bates) (FSM)

Buffalo hide tipi village of Comanche leader Mow Way located a short distance west of Fort Sill in 1873 (Photographer: William S. Soule) (NA)

came to this area from far away, but I never saw any of them.

In 1833, I witnessed a very meaningful event in the skies overhead. It was both wondrous and even scary at the same time! The stars seemed to fall! They say it was a great meteorite shower, and my branches were severely pummeled by the many star fragments dropping from the evening sky. The native people were very much afraid when this happened and they saw it as an omen of things to come. The stories about "the year the stars fell" were recounted around the campfires for a long, long time.

That same year, another significant event occurred a short distance to the northwest in the Wichita Mountains. I recall that a war party from the "Ni-u-ko'n-ska," also known as the Osage, attacked a Kiowa village in a narrow but shallow canyon and killed many people. The victim's heads were removed and placed in brass buckets,

1 Inch

This metallic meteorite was found by the author at the Medicine Bluffs site in 2000. It is very likely from the 1833 meteor shower that was historically noted by the Kiowa as occurring in "the year the stars fell." (Photographer: Lee Gibson) (FSM)

In 1833, the Osage attacked a Kiowa village in the Wichita Mountains, killing many people. The victims' heads were placed in brass buckets or kettles obtained by the Kiowa from the Pawnee shortly before the event. This is one of the buckets from that incident that was associated with the Stumbling Bear family. (Photographer: Lee Gibson) (FSM)

which were then positioned throughout the camp in a symbolic manner. It was a terrible scene, and hereafter this place became known as "Cutthroat Gap" and "Beheading Mountain." The prophecy of the falling stars seemed to have come true.

The First U.S. Dragoons arrived here from Fort Gibson the following year in 1834, bringing with them some captive Kiowa children taken in the Osage raid the year before. This was the first American military expedition to penetrate the southern plains area and make contact with the various groups of native people. The soldiers were weak and sick with fever when they arrived, and they established the first military camp here known as "Camp Comanche" so they could rest and recover.

This first military camp was established near a large Comanche village of approximately six

The First U.S. Dragoons meeting with Comanche warriors under a flag of truce made of white antelope hide, near present-day Fort Sill in 1834 (Artist: George Catlin) (SI)

Top Left: Brigadier General Randolph Marcy, famous soldier and western explorer, as he appeared during the Civil War. Captain Marcy was the first to recommend that a fort be established at Fort Sill when he visited the Medicine Bluffs in 1852. (Photographer: Mathew Brady) (NA)

Top Right: As a soldier with the First U.S. Dragoons Expedition in 1834, Jefferson Davis visited the site where Fort Sill would later be established. He was a West Point graduate, served as a colonel in the Mexican War, was a former U.S. Secretary of War, and a U.S. senator from Mississippi before becoming president of the Confederate States of America during the Civil War. (Engraving from a photograph by Mathew Brady) (NA)

Self-portrait by the famous artist George Catlin, who painted scenes of native people in the vicinity of Camp Comanche (future site of Fort Sill) in 1834 (SI)

hundred tipis, and the native people greeted the soldiers in a warm and friendly manner. The commander of this expedition, General Henry Leavenworth, died before arriving here, and his body was taken back to Fort Gibson for burial. I am told some of the other prominent soldiers in this group were known as Jefferson Davis and Nathan Boone, and they were considered men of great character. Jefferson Davis would later become president of the Confederate States of America. Nathan Boone was the son of Daniel Boone, a famous pioneer who had distinguished himself earlier in the eastern wilderness. Another member of the expedition was a very talented artist by the name of George Catlin. He painted many portraits of the native people while here, and in later years his art was widely recognized as a major contribution to the history of America.

In 1852, I observed the arrival of a second group of American soldiers, who were under the command of Captain Randolph Marcy. The soldiers quickly set up camp around the Medicine Bluffs and began scouting the entire area. They were on a government survey to explore the Red River when they veered north to visit the nearby Wichita Mountains. I remember hearing the captain make a recommendation that a fort should be constructed here. Six years later, another group of native warriors called the "Chicsa" or Chickasaw, under the command of Colonel Douglas Cooper, came to this same area searching for the Comanche. They too suggested this would be an ideal location for the establishment of a military fort.

Colonel Douglas Cooper and his group of Chickasaw "Light-Horsemen" visited the Medicine Bluffs in 1858 and made the second recommendation that a fort be constructed nearby. Cooper later became a prominent Confederate commander of the First Choctaw and Chickasaw Regiment in the Indian Territory during the Civil War. (OHS)

Activities steadily increased in this area after that, and in 1858, another large group of soldiers came from the west in search of the Comanche. Captain Earl Van Dorn and his Texas troops fought a fierce battle with both the Wichita and the Comanche a short distance to the east at a place called Rush Springs. Many of the native people were killed and some captives were taken.

A young lieutenant by the name of Lawrence "Sul" Ross was in charge of the scouts on this expedition, and he successfully rescued a young girl of the light-colored people who was an adopted captive of the Comanche. He soon adopted her as his own daughter and named her "Miss Lizzy." Lieutenant Ross later rose to the rank of brigadier general before leaving the army to become the governor of Texas. "Miss Lizzy" grew up as the governor's daughter and, in 1889, traveled with her stepmother to Los Angeles, California, where she married a wealthy businessman and became the toast of the California social scene. This was a strange journey indeed that had its beginnings near my home on Medicine Bluffs Creek.

Sometime around 1861, it was reported to me that the United States of America suffered a major breakdown, and for four years, two opposing armies were engaged in a terrible struggle with one another. This conflict was referred to variously as the "Civil War," the "War Between the States," or the "War of the Rebellion," and it did great harm to the unity of the nation. Representatives of both armies frequently visited this area and held councils with all of the tribes in an effort to enlist their support during this difficult period. Some of the native people who lived east of here, the Chickasaw, Choctaw, Creek, Seminole, and the Cherokee, heavily supported the Southern army, and they were engaged in many battles during this conflict.

It was a time of great turmoil, and no one knew whom to trust. Most of the native people in this area tried to stay out of the war as they regarded both sides with great suspicion. In 1862, the soldiers from Texas attempted to establish a fortified block house near my home at the edge of the Wichita Mountains and call it "Camp Beauregard." However, they failed in this effort, and I was glad when this conflict finally ended in 1865.

The Diary: The Formative Years

In the winter of 1868, soldiers swept down from the Kansas area north of here and attacked a village of the Cheyenne or "Tsistsista" people on the Washita River. Native people from my area were also camped nearby on the Washita River at that time. It was a bloody encounter resulting in many casualties among the Cheyenne and Arapaho people, and I was very dismayed to hear of this conflict so close to my home. The Comanche and Kiowa people were not far from the battle site and went to assist the Cheyenne, prompting the soldiers to quickly return north to Camp Supply, leaving some of their soldiers behind and unaccounted for.

Colonel Benjamin Grierson and the Tenth U.S. Cavalry conducting a reconnaissance at the Medicine Bluffs in December 1868 (Photographer: William S. Soule) (NA)

However, a short time later, the soldiers returned to the Washita River accompanied by reinforcements to bury the dead they had left behind and also to search for other missing soldiers. The missing soldiers, including Major Joel Elliot, had also been killed by the native people, and their bodies had to be buried as well. Decisions were soon made to come even farther south to the Wichita Mountains and establish a new army post on the Medicine Bluffs Creek. To my surprise, the soldiers began erecting their tents and constructing temporary shelters in dugouts immediately adjacent to my home on the creek. They were everywhere! While I was somewhat concerned about my safety, it was also interesting to observe these new activities. This temporary camp was initially known as "Camp Wichita" or "Camp on Medicine Bluffs Creek."

Many of these reinforcement soldiers were very dark in color, and they were sometimes referred to as "Buffalo Soldiers." They were actually the Tenth U.S. Cavalry under the command of a light-colored officer by the name of Colonel Benjamin Grierson. Ironically, these dark-colored soldiers were former slaves of the light-colored people and had only recently been given their freedom following the Civil War. They were now establishing their independence and reliability in a new military context.

I have learned that Colonel Grierson was well known in the military for his brave and gallant exploits during the Civil War where he held the rank of brevet brigadier general. It was my understanding that like many of the officers who remained in the army following that event, he went back to his permanent rank of colonel when he came west. I took note of Grierson's beard and was told by the wise old owl that he had been kicked in the face by a horse when he was young and the beard made him feel more comfortable about his appearance. It was also interesting to note that he had been a musician before the war and was now a cavalry commander.

The light-colored soldiers who had earlier fought on the Washita River were the Seventh U.S. Cavalry under the command of Lieutenant Colonel George A. Custer, and they were quickly joined by the Nineteenth Kansas Volunteers under the command of Governor Samuel J. Crawford. The Kansas Volunteers were a temporary army of "Indian Fighters" that had been recruited to support the Seventh Cavalry during the "Winter War" campaign of 1868 in the Indian Territory.

Custer also was a well-known military hero from the Civil War, having led eleven separate cavalry charges in battle. As a result of his flamboyant and daring exploits, Custer was

Civil War view of Brevet Brigadier General George A. Custer. Lieutenant Colonel Custer commanded the Seventh U.S. Cavalry during the "Winter War" on the southern plains in 1868 and was stationed at Fort Sill from December 1868 to March 1869. Later, he also participated in the army investigation at Fort Sill regarding the scandal for issuing permits to Indian traders. (NA)

featured in many national newspapers of the day. Like Grierson, he held a temporary rank of brevet brigadier general during the war but later reverted to his permanent rank of lieutenant colonel. I had no difficulty identifying him since he was well known for his curly blond hair, his distinctive uniform, and his commanding attitude and manner. His brother Tom was also a highly decorated soldier, who had earned the Medal of Honor on two separate occasions, and I often saw him talking with his brother George around the camp or along the creek.

Two of Custer's subordinate officers, Major Marcus Reno and Captain Frederick Benteen, were present at Camp Wichita as well. These two officers were not very happy with Custer, and I occasionally overheard discussions in camp

The new army post was named by General Sheridan in honor of his West Point classmate, Brigadier General Joshua Sill, who was killed during the Civil War at Stone River, Tennessee, in 1862. (NA)

about him leaving Major Elliott and his men behind at the Washita River battle earlier. In fact, I witnessed a confrontation between Benteen and Custer one day over this very issue, and I thought someone was going to be killed. Despite the threat, the incident passed without violence. I was told later that these old resentments were still a problem when they were all engaged with the native people far to the north at the Little Bighorn in the spring of 1876, where Custer and much of his command were killed. Ironically, Benteen was later promoted to brevet brigadier general and returned in 1884–1885 to become the commander of Fort Sill.

Both the dark- and light-colored soldiers began to construct a permanent fort on the little plateau south of Medicine Bluffs Creek, and January 8, 1869, was officially considered the founding date for the new army post. This was the same location where a large village of the Wichita native people had existed many years before. I overheard the senior officer, General Philip H. Sheridan, make a decision to name the fledgling military post "Fort Sill," and by the summer of that same year, the War Department had approved the name. Sheridan named the post after his West Point classmate, Brigadier General Joshua Sill, who had been killed at a place called Stone River, Tennessee, in 1862 during the Civil War. Colonel

Far Left: The first post commander of Fort Sill was Colonel Benjamin Grierson, who was also the commander of the Tenth U.S. Cavalry Regiment and a Civil War hero. This view of Brevet Brigadier General Grierson was taken during the Civil War. (NA)

Left: General Philip H. Sheridan was commander of the Department of Missouri when he drove the first stake in the ground to establish a permanent military post at Fort Sill on January 8, 1869. (NA)

Grierson was selected by General Sheridan to build and command the newly established post on Medicine Bluffs Creek.

There was a frenzy of activity around here beginning early in 1869. Log and stone buildings were springing up everywhere on the little plateau just south of me. Some soldiers camped along the creek nearby, and their constant chatter disturbed the quiet in the forest, causing the animals to move away. Men on horses passed by occasionally, and sometimes they stopped to rest and eat their meals under the shade of my massive canopy. I worried when the soldiers used their sharp axes on my trunk and branches in an effort to obtain fuel for their campfires. Some of the scars from these wounds are still visible on my trunk today. I was very lucky to have survived those days!

Historic axe marks from the distant past are still visible on the trunk of the Silent Witness bur oak tree. (Photographer: Jetawn Spivey) (AUTH)

The construction of the stone buildings at Fort Sill by soldiers and civilian "mechanics" from Kansas was fully underway in 1870. This view is toward the southeast of the east line of family quarters. (Photographer: William S. Soule) (FSM)

Some of the people who came with the soldiers dressed and acted very differently. These individuals served as scouts for the army, and oddly enough, they came from both the light-colored and the native people. They had been in this country before and knew where the best campsites and sources of water were located, as well as where the groups of native people were usually camped. The soldiers depended heavily on these scouts to avoid danger and keep them from getting lost.

One of the unusual characters who came to this area very early was a light-colored man with a red beard. He was a trader by the name of William Matthewson, and I heard that he was very experienced and had traveled far and wide throughout the western part of the country before coming to the Medicine Bluffs. Matthewson had earned a reputation as a great buffalo hunter. Many people referred to him as "Buffalo Bill" Matthewson because he had saved a lot of lives during a harsh winter in Kansas by killing large numbers of buffalo to feed the light-colored people in that area. The native people referred to him as "Terrible Red Bearded Man" as he was also known to have a temper. He soon established a log trading post just southeast of the new fort where he provided many necessary items to the native people. Matthewson became very wealthy from his trading activities and eventually returned to Kansas to become one of the leading citizens in the city of Wichita.

I regularly noticed one of the light-colored people walking around with a box on a tripod and periodically stopping to set the tripod down before pointing it at various subjects. Sometimes he pointed it at the soldiers, other times at the native people and their villages. I observed him pointing his box at the Medicine Bluffs on many occasions. I learned later that he was William S. Soule, a photographer who had originally come from a village far to the northeast known as Boston, Massachusetts. Soule was the first person to take photographs in this area, and I learned a lot from watching him, but I never understood how he captured an image of the people and the scenery just by pointing his box at them.

Early in 1869, I observed another interesting activity among these soldiers. In the winter of that year the men of the Seventh U.S. Cavalry and the Nineteenth Kansas Volunteers would regularly play a game I had never seen before.

Soldiers of the Seventh Cavalry and the Nineteenth Kansas Volunteers first began playing organized "base ball" at Fort Sill in January to March 1869. This image of a nineteenth-century baseball game was taken on the southwest corner of the parade ground at a time when home plate had been temporarily relocated near the flagpole in the center of the parade ground. Normally the reverse was true, with home plate located at the southwest corner. (FSM)

They would form a square or diamond with one player positioned in the center and one at each corner. The central player would throw a ball to one corner of the diamond, and the player at that location would attempt to strike it with a wooden bat before running past each of the other three corners.

It took a while for me to understand what the running and shouting was all about. They called it "base ball," and I understand this was the first time it had been played in an organized manner within the bounds of what would later become the state of Oklahoma. It is also curious to note that more than eighty years later, in 1951, a very famous baseball player by the name of Mickey Mantle would take his physical examination for the army at Fort Sill.

The cluster of stone buildings continued to expand in the early years of the fort, but in 1870 the soldiers were still very vulnerable to attack by the native people, who saw them as invading their territory. The temporary horse corral made of wooden rails was a prime target for the native people to steal the army horses, and many were lost in this early period. During that year the soldiers finally constructed a more permanent corral with high stone walls, penetrated by small portholes at the right height to fire their weapons through. The only entrance to the corral was a double gate on the west side.

Because of this added security, Kiowa and Cheyenne raiders changed their tactics and decided to steal the horses at a different location where they were less secure. Each day, I watched as the soldiers took the horses to graze on the large open prairie south of the fort. At noon, the guards would come into the post to eat, leaving only a few behind to protect the herd. This was the time Big Tree, the Kiowa leader of this raid, chose to take all of the cavalry horses at Fort Sill in one sweep, thus exceeding any similar raid in the past.

The native people divided into two groups, one to remain on the northwest side of the post

An unidentified cavalry soldier with his horse at Fort Sill in the 1880s. Many cavalry units were stationed at Fort Sill over time, including the Fourth, Fifth, Seventh, Ninth, and Tenth regiments. The last cavalry troop left Fort Sill in 1907 and was replaced by infantry and artillery. (FSM)

near Signal Mountain, while the other moved eastward following Medicine Bluffs Creek to take position on the southeast side of the post along East Cache Creek. At the precise moment during the noon meal, the two groups planned to attack by sweeping south around the post in a pincer-like fashion and hit the herd in the large pasture. The element of surprise was very important, and I was most curious to see if this plan would work.

Unfortunately for the native people, before the eastern group could get into position, the western group encountered some Texas woodcutters sleeping in their tents on the prairie, a target so tempting they could not resist. One Texan was killed and scalped in this incident. The resulting gunfire attracted the attention of Joseph Chandler, a horse trader who lived in a nearby dugout with his wife Tomasa, a former Comanche captive. Chandler immediately warned the post of the attack, but the army was slow to respond.

Immediately following this incident, the eastern group attacked a separate herd of horses guarded by Texas and Mexican cowboys, killing one unfortunate person in the process. With the alert being sounded, the soldiers guarding the horse herd in the big pasture south of Fort Sill did not leave the herd as expected. Big Tree decided that the element of surprise was lost by the attack on the Texans, and the plan for the greatest horse-stealing raid against the army failed.

As my leaves began to unfurl in the spring of 1871, word came about an incident in front of the commander's quarters on the north side of the little cluster of stone buildings. Almost all of the army's commanding generals came to Fort Sill to investigate why the native people were raiding from Fort Sill into Texas. General William Tecumseh Sherman called for a conference with the Kiowa people on the front porch of the house. Amid much tension and suspicion, some of the Kiowa leaders attempted to kill the senior leader

General William T. Sherman narrowly escaped death several times at Fort Sill while holding council with Kiowa warriors on the front porch of the post commander's quarters in May 1871. As a result, the house was soon dubbed "Sherman House" by the eastern newspapers. (NA)

of the army. They were unsuccessful, however, and some of the Kiowa leaders were arrested and confined in the basement beneath the cavalry barracks before being taken back to Texas for trial and punishment.

Satank ("Set-tain'ga"), Satanta ("Se-tain'te") and Big Tree ("Addo-eetee") were to be escorted by the Fourth U.S. Cavalry from Fort Sill to Fort Richardson, Texas, to stand trial for murder in the court of the light-colored people. However, Satank was killed a short distance south of the fort while trying to escape, as he did not want to go to a Texas prison.

The other two prominent Kiowa war leaders, Satanta and Big Tree, were taken to Texas and, after being found guilty of murder, were confined in the State Prison at Huntsville. General Sherman returned to his headquarters in Washington, D.C., and the stone house where he stayed during this turbulent visit to Fort Sill became well known in the newspapers back east after this as "Sherman House."

Both Satanta and Big Tree were well known in the southern plains. Satanta was a veteran of many battles in Texas and Kansas, and he often blew a bugle he had taken in combat from a Kansas soldier. Many Texans trembled in fear during an attack when they heard the distinctive blare of his bugle. He was also known as the "Orator of the Plains" for his passionate speech made during the negotiations in the 1867 Treaty of Medicine Lodge, Kansas, among others. Big Tree was the youngest of the three warriors, but he had already distinguished himself in battle many times before being sent to the Texas prison.

Satanta and Big Tree were paroled back to Fort Sill in 1873, and owing to confusion and conflicting authorities between the military and civilian governments pertaining to the native people, the army soon freed them. After a while they were arrested again for new offenses and returned to the Texas prison to serve out their original life sentence. In 1878, Satanta was killed in an incident at the prison, and eventually Big Tree was paroled back to Fort Sill a second time. Big Tree was later converted to Christianity and became a minister in the church of the light-colored people and a teacher for the native children at a place called "Rainy Mountain." This series of circumstances was very surprising to me!

Satank became the first of the native people to be buried in the Post Cemetery at Fort Sill, and the remains of Satanta were later moved by his family from the Texas prison to the Fort Sill cemetery as well. Today, they are surrounded by the remains of many other important warrior-leaders in a special area of high honor in the Post Cemetery, often referred to as "Chief's Knoll" or the "Indian Arlington." I can easily see this hallowed ground from my place on Medicine Bluffs Creek.

Conflict between the army and the native people continued to escalate, and during 1874–1875 there was all-out war on the southern plains. This conflict was referred to as the "Red River War" or the "Buffalo War," and it signaled a major change for the native people. Some of the great warriors like Quanah ("Quinah") Parker, Wild Horse ("Kobay-o-bura"), Kicking Bird ("Tay-nay-an-gopte"), Lone Wolf ("Gui-pah-go"), and Making Medicine surrendered or were taken prisoner at the fort, and it became necessary for their people to depend on the government for food and shelter after this.

Quanah surrendered in the late spring of 1875, and in his words, "…followed the wolf and the eagle into Fort Sill." I watched as he passed my home on Medicine Bluffs Creek that spring

The Quahada Comanche war leader "Quinah" (Quanah Parker) led the attack on the buffalo hunters at Adobe Walls in 1874 and also fought in other engagements against the army on the southern plains before surrendering at Fort Sill in June of 1875. He and his mother, white captive Cynthia Ann Parker, as well as his sister Prairie Flower, are buried on Chief's Knoll in the Post Cemetery. (Photographer: W. P. Bliss) (NA)

"Se-tain'te" or Satanta, also known as "White Bear," the prominent Kiowa war leader, was confined in the Post Guardhouse several times but continued to fight his enemies until 1878 when he was killed in the Texas State Prison at Huntsville. He is buried on Chief's Knoll in the Post Cemetery at Fort Sill. (Photographer: William S. Soule) (FSM)

on his way into the fort area. He was the son of the white captive Cynthia Ann Parker and a great Comanche warrior named "Peta Nacona." Quanah was destined to become a great leader himself for both the native people and the light-colored people in the years to come.

Certain of the more troublesome warriors and families were kept in the newly constructed icehouse before being sent to prison in a far-off place called Florida. The roof had not been constructed at that time, and the vertical stone walls, absent of windows, stood in stark contrast along the sloping landscape to the east of the officers' quarters. Tipis were set up inside the icehouse to provide maximum protection from the weather, with the stone walls serving as an effective windbreak. The upper portion of these conical-shaped tipis penetrated the open sky above the stone walls, and the tips of the poles fanned haphazardly upward and outward like so many extended fingers reaching out in desperation.

The primary purpose, however, was to restrict the men and their families from leaving the area. They were very cramped, and I could not help but feel sorry for them. The soldiers stood guard around this rectangular stone building, and they were very much afraid of a breakout by the prisoners within. When it was time to feed the prisoners, they would throw raw meat over the stone walls rather than enter the building and risk their own lives. The smoke from cooking fires within the building could be seen rising gently in the sky throughout the days and nights.

The quartermaster's stone corral was also used as a temporary prison for these native people during this time. This was the initial gathering place where the fierce warriors and their families were counted and recorded. It was here that the weapons and horses were taken from them so they could not make war again. Many of these weapons were stacked high in the center of the open plaza and burned while some were taken as souvenirs by the soldiers. Following this activity, they were

assigned camp areas around the perimeter of Fort Sill and they would promptly move to those sites and begin erecting their tipis.

After a while, the Kiowa, Comanche, Plains Apache, Cheyenne, and Arapaho warriors confined in the icehouse were loaded onto wagons to begin a long journey east to a place called Florida, where they were again imprisoned in a much larger stone fort along the seacoast at Fort Marion near St. Augustine. It would be more than two long years before these warriors returned to their loved ones along the Medicine Bluffs Creek and in the surrounding Wichita Mountains. They had many fascinating stories to tell of unfamiliar scenes and activities they had experienced during their journey to the world of the light-colored people.

I have recently heard that one of the Cheyenne warriors taken to the Florida prison was Making Medicine. He eventually converted to the Christian faith and, after two years in prison, went to New York before returning to this country a short time later. In the meantime, he took a new name, "David Pendleton Oakerhater," after his Episcopalian mentor, reflecting his intense interest in a new way of life. Long after his death he was recognized as the first native saint in the Episcopal Church of the light-colored people. His efforts in establishing a mission among the fierce Cheyenne of the Indian Territory, under very difficult circumstances and with virtually no assistance from the Episcopal Church, were outstanding. This series of events was nothing short of astonishing to me!

With the surrenders of the native people at Fort Sill following the Red River War in 1874–1875, the responsibility for feeding these former warriors and buffalo hunters fell to the government, or more precisely, the Indian Agency. I was told that President U. S. Grant had appointed Quakers from the midwestern part of the country as Indian agents because he felt their strong religious beliefs ensured they would

Making Medicine, also known as "David Pendleton Oakerhater," was a Cheyenne warrior who surrendered at Fort Sill in 1875 and subsequently was sent to prison at Fort Marion, Florida. After leaving prison, he spent time studying with the Episcopal Church in New York before returning to the Indian Territory and establishing an Episcopal mission. Years later, in honor of his exceptional service under extraordinary circumstances, the church recognized this warrior/minister as the first Native American Anglican saint. (GH)

treat the native people honestly and fairly. They wanted the native people to become farmers instead of the buffalo hunters and warriors they had always been. I could see that this was a daunting task and filled with problems that would not be easily overcome. Lawrie Tatum, the first Quaker agent, made a valiant effort, but it was obvious that the agents did not understand the native people very well.

However, everyone understood that hunger was a primary reason that could cause the native warriors to once again take up arms and resume raiding into Texas or Mexico. On two occasions

I recall, the supplies were late in arriving at the agency south of Fort Sill, and the post commander had to step in to prevent a disaster from happening. He ordered the post bakery to operate twenty-four hours a day producing freshly baked bread for issue to the native people, just to carry them through the immediate crisis. The native people had never tasted baked bread before and they loved it. They referred to it as "soldier bread," and it was eagerly sought by the hungry warriors and their families. It was pleasing to see the army's expression of concern for the common good.

The agency supplies soon arrived, but the agent withheld the rations for a while longer to ensure the native people remained on the reservation. This was very unsettling for the tribes but the agency forced them into compliance. In the meantime, however, the threat of war had been averted by loaves of freshly baked bread.

In the old days I often noticed that the native people did not care for the same foods as the light-colored people. These warrior/hunters were accustomed to a steady diet of buffalo, deer, or antelope meat. But I also noticed that some of them did not like to eat the meat from the bears that lived in the mountains since there were taboos against doing this. However, the prairie dogs and wolf pups were considered very tasty. Turkey or prairie chickens were generally frowned upon since they were regarded as cowards when they suddenly flew up in front of the hunters, making much noise in the process. Fish or other animals from the creeks were generally not considered appealing either. Although they did not eat many vegetables, certain roots and berries they often encountered on the prairies and among the bushes in the forests were prized as food.

Some of the foods that the government agency of the light-colored people provided to these native people did not agree with their traditional tastes. The cloth sacks of flour, sugar, and coffee were quickly accepted and favored. The light-colored people also provided rice in cloth sacks, but the natives looked on this food with disgust. It reminded them of maggots, and they would quickly dump the rice onto the ground and save the cloth sacks for other purposes.

For several years after the native people surrendered at Fort Sill, the agency provided cattle purchased from the Texas herds as they journeyed north up the Chisholm Trail. The cattle were considered a substitute for the buffalo the native people were so used to. Once a month, they would gather around a large log corral on East Cache Creek, a short distance to the east, where the cattle were issued "on the hoof." This permitted the native people to chase the cattle before killing them.

This gathering was a time of great celebration, and the men eagerly anticipated the big hunt. When the corral gate was opened and the cattle stampeded out one or two at a time and ran down the valley, the individual warriors mounted their horses and gave chase with much yelling and fanfare. It was very exciting to watch as they rode hard for a mile or so before delivering the final bullet or arrow to kill the steer. The thrill of the chase and the final killing of these wild Texas cattle was the next best thing to hunting the buffalo. The native women quickly moved in and began the butchering process to recover and use almost every part of the animal as they had always done with the buffalo in the past.

After a few years, however, the wives of the light-colored officers at Fort Sill began to complain loudly. I heard them refer to this prolonged chase of the Texas steers as "barbaric." They felt it would be more efficient if the cattle were simply killed in the corral in the same way as the light-colored people did. Soon the agency changed their

A Comanche family in the process of butchering a recently killed Texas steer issued on the hoof at Fort Sill in 1892. Every part of the animal was consumed or used for some purpose. (Photographer: James Mooney) (NA)

methods and began issuing the beef to the native people already butchered and wrapped in brown paper tied with string. Instead of chasing and killing the cattle, round brass tokens or medals of different denominations were issued to the native people to be redeemed at the agency store for various amounts of beef (two, five, ten, twenty, or fifty pounds). I do not believe the light-colored women fully realized that they were taking away the final element of the big hunts from the old days and the native people were losing more than they gained in this effort to be helpful.

Some of the dark-colored people in the Tenth U.S. Cavalry left Fort Sill in 1874, but other light-colored soldiers of the Fourth U.S. Cavalry under Colonel Ranald Mackenzie arrived from Texas around this time and took charge of the fort. Mackenzie was a bachelor who was known as the great "Indian Fighter." Another bachelor named Horace P. Jones was a very experienced scout and interpreter, and during these turbulent times, he sometimes stayed in the same house with Mackenzie so he would be available on short notice to interpret what the native people were saying. Jones had many hunting dogs, and they were constantly barking at something. Not only the commander's neighbors, but also the animals in the forest were very irritated with this continual noise.

One of the more interesting light-colored soldiers that I observed at Fort Sill over a period of years was an officer by the name of Captain George Schofield. Schofield was very active with the native people during the Red River War, and he had also served as commander of the post seven different times when called upon to do so during the absence of other commanders. He invented a special revolver while stationed at Fort Sill and field tested it in combat for the Smith & Wesson Firearms Company located in Springfield, Massachusetts.

I was told that he frequently fought battles with the Comanche and Kiowa around Fort Sill using his special .45-caliber "Schofield" revolver and would relay the numbers of casualties and captives to the firearms company in the hopes the army would officially adopt it as a standard weapon for the cavalry. He ultimately failed in this effort and was so distraught when he left Fort Sill in 1879 that he committed suicide with his Schofield revolver soon after arriving in Fort Bowie, Arizona.

In 1875, I watched as some of the soldiers came to the creek and dug up a number of small trees for transplanting around the little square where the stone buildings had been built. I was puzzled by this activity since the soldiers had earlier been cutting down so many trees. Now they seemed to reverse their behavior and began planting trees in specific areas under the direction of Colonel Mackenzie. They seemed to prefer the hackberry tree, and they spaced the trees evenly apart in a nice straight row around the square and also along the opposite side of the streets. The soldiers watered the young trees regularly, although they did not seem to enjoy it very much. I appreciated their efforts, however, since I would now have greater opportunities for keeping up with the news from the fledgling army post.

The soldiers regularly came to the creek for other purposes as well. During the mid- to late winter, all available soldiers would gather at the creek to harvest the ice that had formed on the surface of the frigid waters. Timing was critical, and they always seemed to know when the circumstances were just right. When the ice was at least four inches thick, many soldiers would appear carrying large toothed saws, drills, and sharp axes to cut the ice into blocks, which were then loaded onto wagons.

This was very hard and chilling work, but they seemed to make light of it at times, particularly when the families accompanied them to watch the activities and play along the snow-covered banks or on the glazed, slippery surface of the ice. They seemed to have a good time throwing snowballs at one another and even skating on the hard blue ice. But after a while, the bitter cold became too much, and everyone quickly disappeared.

The horse-drawn ice wagons eventually made their short journey up the creek bank to the stone icehouse located along the sloping hillside immediately east of the houses. Here the large blocks of ice were unloaded and neatly stacked for ready access at a later date. With sawdust from the sawmill used for packing and insulation, there would still be ice available well into the summer for everyone to drink a sweet-and-sour-tasting liquid called "lemonade" on special occasions. This seemed like a lot of hard work in very cold weather just to drink something cold during hot weather.

Ever since the first buildings had been constructed at the little fort, I had noticed a lot of unusual activity around some of the smaller buildings behind the barracks. There were women of many different cultural backgrounds washing the clothes and bedsheets of the soldiers and hanging them out to dry on rope lines or across stacks of firewood. These very busy women were known as "laundresses," and they seemed to be extremely independent in their behavior. I witnessed some of them having arguments with the soldiers on occasion, and one of them became so irate that she used a bullwhip to express her unhappiness with his behavior. Many of them even married the soldiers, and soon there were children running all around behind the barracks. Strange things sometimes happened when people were isolated on the wild frontier!

The wives of the officers did not care for the laundresses, and they seldom spoke to one another. It was not uncommon to witness a chance encounter between them when walking along the boardwalks in front of the buildings. They would totally ignore one another until they had passed, and then each would turn in a very subtle fashion and stare at the other's backside. The squirrels thought it was so funny one time when we saw an officer's wife trip over a wheelbarrow while walking forward and looking backward at the same time.

By 1878, this stressful relationship reached a breaking point, and the officers' wives were complaining in high places. Official hearings were held to determine the fate of the laundresses throughout the army and there was much concern about the outcome of this meeting. Some considered the laundresses immoral, and they were accused of having a bad influence on the soldiers. Others stated the laundresses provided "a motherly influence" to the soldiers while also serving as "angels of mercy" during epidemics and disasters. When all was said and done, it was decided the laundresses would be terminated throughout the army with the exception of those who were currently married to soldiers. However, as the soldier-husbands left the army, the washerwomen would not be replaced, and by 1885 there were no more laundresses in the army. This situation caused major problems in getting the laundry done, and the dirty clothes really began to pile up after that.

I was intrigued to learn one day in 1875 that the soldiers had installed a new system of communication called a "telegraph." A continuing line of poles or trees without limbs, having connecting vines or wires stretching from top to top, were planted in the ground extending north from Fort Richardson, Texas, and across the Red River to Fort Sill. Somehow messages were sent and received over great distances using this peculiar system of poles and wires. Some of the native people referred to the telegraph lines as "singing wires," and the written messages were often called "talking leaves."

In the hot summer of 1879 this telegraph system was supplemented by the first telephone in what would later become Oklahoma. Now the soldiers could actually speak directly to one another over great distances. Since in the beginning, no one else in the Indian Territory had this equipment, there was no one to talk to, and it could only be used to communicate with the light-colored people in Texas.

But soon, a second telephone was installed at the Darlington Indian Agency near Fort Reno, followed by the third telephone at Fort Supply farther to the northwest. The soldiers at Fort Reno began constructing a telephone line south toward Fort Sill while soldiers from the latter post also initiated a new line extending north toward Fort Reno. They would ultimately connect somewhere along the way between the two army posts. I was told that the Comanche leader Quanah Parker actually listened on the telephone at Fort Sill while a soldier at Fort Reno blew the bugle into his telephone. He was very impressed when he heard the bugle from more than eighty miles away. I was somewhat skeptical about this whole situation, and I still think the grapevine actually works better.

I had grown accustomed to seeing the soldiers moving about the post area in the four-wheeled wagons drawn by several horses or mules. But I also took note of a special kind of horse-drawn wagon that came first from the east, and later from the north, and finally from the south, to carry more people to and from Fort Sill. I heard these special wagons referred to as "stagecoaches" and sometimes as "mud wagons," and I was fascinated by their uniqueness.

These blocky-looking, enclosed wagons had windows and doors unlike the other wagons I was used to seeing. Over time, I came to understand more about these stagecoaches. The officers and their wives, Deputy U.S. Marshals, businessmen, very important politicians, and other travelers regularly came to, and left from, Fort Sill on the stagecoach. In the beginning, a stagecoach arrived weekly from the little settlement of Caddo, Indian Territory, located on the Butterfield or Overland Stage Road about three days' hard ride east of Fort Sill. Rush Springs was the last stop before arriving at Fort Sill.

Early stagecoach travel to and from Fort Sill is illustrated by the woodcut engraving *Meeting with the Old Regiment* by R. F. Zogbaum from *Harper's Weekly* magazine, June 7, 1890. (AUTH)

I noticed the wording "El Paso Stage Lines" painted on the side of the wagons above the doors and windows. The squirrels explained to me that this company had received a contract from the Overland Stage Lines to deliver travelers to Fort Sill. Later, I heard this company was reorganized into the "Southwestern Stage Lines," but it was still based out of El Paso, Texas. There was nothing west of Fort Sill, so the stagecoach had to turn around and return to Caddo each trip.

Stagecoaches also began arriving from the north passing through Caldwell, the last town in Kansas, before entering the Indian Territory, through Pond Creek to Fort Reno, and finally arriving at Fort Sill. There were signs posted along the stage road at the Kansas state line near Caldwell proclaiming the last chance to drink whiskey before entering the Indian Territory. Possession of alcohol in the Indian Territory was serious business and a criminal offense for anyone caught by the Deputy U.S. Marshals.

Eventually, another stagecoach route opened up when the road extended north from Henrietta, Texas, across Red River into the Indian Territory before finally arriving at Fort Sill. All of this traveling to and from Fort Sill made my limbs twist. It was obvious that improved communications and transportation were having an effect on the local activities. Both mail and passengers were being transported faster and in ways unknown to this part of the country before.

One of these stagecoach travelers from the east was Lieutenant Henry O. Flipper, a dark-colored soldier who would rise to great prominence as the first of his people to graduate from the West Point Military Academy. Originally from Georgia, Lieutenant Flipper came directly from West Point to St. Louis, where he took the Overland Stage Line to Caddo, Indian Territory, before arriving at Fort Sill for his first duty assignment in 1877. Surprisingly, he experienced very little prejudice from either the light-colored officers or the other dark-colored soldiers stationed at the post.

Indeed, he made many friends while serving at Fort Sill.

Lieutenant Flipper's first duty assignment at Fort Sill was to serve as the Officer of the Day, and when he first reported to the guardhouse, he was confronted with a very awkward situation. The post commander's son was being held there as a result of his own general order. A few days before, the post commander had issued orders that anyone caught walking on the grass of the parade ground would be arrested and confined in the guardhouse. The first person arrested was the commander's own son.

Flipper went to the commander's quarters to discuss this delicate situation, but upon approaching the front door he overheard a very intense and even heated discussion about the

In 1877, Lieutenant Henry O. Flipper was the first African American to graduate from the West Point Military Academy. His first duty station after leaving West Point was at Fort Sill, Indian Territory, from 1877 to 1879. (NA)

boy between the commander and his wife in the front parlor. The commander explained that he had to set an example in this case and could not show favoritism toward his own son. This was unsatisfactory to the commander's wife. Impatiently, he stated in a loud commanding voice, "Madam, I'll have you know I am the commander of this post." The equally strong response from his wife was, "Sir, I'll have you know I am your commander—get my son out of there." Flipper did not bother to knock on the door but instead returned to the guardhouse and released the boy, thus restoring peace to Fort Sill.

He was also responsible for planning and constructing an extensive drainage ditch just west of my shaded area. Although there were those who initially doubted the success of his ditch, when the rains came the following spring, the flood waters from Medicine Bluffs Creek drained back to the creek as intended. This drainage ditch eliminated a large swampy area that had been a major health hazard for the post, and I was so glad to see those pesky mosquitoes go away!

But alas, in the fall of 1879, Lieutenant Flipper received orders for a new assignment at Fort Elliott, Texas. As he traveled west on the road past the Medicine Bluffs and near my home along the creek, I saw him turn and look back at the little cluster of stone buildings. In that brief but emotional moment, I witnessed him weeping like a child. He hated to leave Fort Sill! It was a very touching moment and I really missed him after that.

On frequent occasions, I saw the soldiers leaving the fort to pursue the many outlaws in this vicinity. These very bad people included horse and mule rustlers, deserters, whiskey peddlers, thieves, and murderers. Many of these bad men lived in the Indian Territory but others came all the way from Kansas, Texas, and Mexico just to kill and steal from other people. Some outlaws were caught traveling north with the large herds of cattle moving along the Chisholm Trail from Texas to Kansas just thirty miles east of my home. The army was on constant alert for these outlaws, and they successfully brought many of them to justice.

Additional troops of cavalry and infantry arrived at Fort Sill during this time to contend with these lawbreakers. Some of the dark-colored soldiers of the Tenth U.S. Cavalry stationed at Fort Sill were soon joined or replaced by other dark-colored soldiers of the Ninth U.S. Cavalry, as well as the Twenty-fourth and Twenty-fifth Infantry. These were all of the dark-colored regiments in the U.S. Army, later referred to collectively as "Buffalo Soldiers," and they performed magnificently in maintaining law and order in the Indian Territory.

There were many "Intruders" who came into the Territory illegally to try and take the land away from the native people. Some of these "Intruders" were referred to as "Boomers" since they deliberately broke the law while publicly campaigning for the government to change the laws and make these lands available for settlement by the light-colored people. A man by the name of David Payne led many of these "Boomers" into various parts of the Indian Territory, and I frequently saw him around Fort Sill. He had been a soldier with the Nineteenth Kansas Volunteers when they came here to establish Fort Sill in the very beginning.

After returning to Kansas in early 1869, he later became known as "Captain David Payne— King of the Boomers" for his many efforts to force the government to change the laws by publicly disobeying them. "Captain" Payne returned to the Indian Territory many times as a civilian attempting to illegally establish settlements or "colonies." He was arrested by the army several different times and confined in the stone guardhouse at Fort Sill. On one occasion the soldiers escorted him out of the Indian Territory toward Texas and abandoned him in the middle of the Red River. He promptly turned around and re-entered the Territory again to continue disobeying the law. He was a very stubborn man!

Ejecting an Oklahoma Boomer. Buffalo Soldiers of the Ninth and Tenth U.S. Cavalry from Fort Sill were frequently engaged in removing illegal settlers from the Indian Territory, as seen in this engraving from *Harpers Weekly* dated March 28, 1885. (Sketched by T. de Thulstrup with final by Frederic Remington) (FSM)

Eventually, the continued efforts of the "Boomers" succeeded, and the laws were changed to permit settlement at specific times, in specific areas. As the official land openings began in the spring of 1889, many settlers who came to be known as "Sooners" tried to sneak in earlier than they were supposed to and stake a claim on the land. The soldiers were always arresting these "Boomers" and "Sooners," or at least attempting to chase them out of the Territory. Many of these "Intruders" were temporarily confined within the walls of the quartermaster corral, where the native people had likewise been imprisoned a few short years before.

In 1875, a very wise and powerful man by the name of Judge Isaac C. Parker assumed control of the federal court in Fort Smith, Arkansas, with jurisdiction over Fort Sill and the Indian Territory. He sent many Deputy U.S. Marshals across the Indian Territory to help the army enforce the law in this violent land where it was often said "there was no law west of Fort Smith." It was brought to my attention once that during the two-hundred-year history of the U.S. Marshals Service (1789–1989), approximately 350 of these brave men were killed in the line of duty throughout the United States.

Deputy U.S. Marshal Jimmie Jones (left) and army scout (later marshal) Jack Stilwell (right) at Fort Sill in 1874–1875. Jones served both as a Deputy U.S. Marshal under the famous "Hanging Judge" Isaac Parker and as an army scout at Fort Sill. Stilwell was the hero of the Beecher's Island battle in eastern Colorado between Major Forsyth's Fifth Cavalry and Cheyenne warriors under Roman Nose. Jack's brother Frank Stilwell also spent time at Fort Sill and was later killed by Wyatt Earp in Tucson, Arizona, following the gunfight at the OK Corral in Tombstone. (Photographer: W. P. Bliss) (RM)

Almost half of that number were killed in the wild country that later became known as Oklahoma.

Judge Parker's court was not subject to the U.S. Supreme Court initially but only to the President of the United States. Parker quickly became known as the "Hanging Judge," and he was responsible for hanging eighty-eight bad people at Fort Smith. Several prisoners from the Fort Sill guardhouse were among those who received justice on his gallows. This large wooden gallows was built to accommodate six people at a time, and the trapdoors beneath their feet were frequently referred to as "the Gates to Hell."

Sometime around 1888, I noticed a rather unusual man of the light-colored people moving around the post and the villages of the native people carrying one of those camera boxes, as well as sketchpads, framed canvas, and a wooden tripod

Soldiers stand on the front porch of the post guardhouse built in 1872. Many Native American warriors, soldiers, and civilian outlaws were confined in this jail until a new guardhouse was built elsewhere on the post in 1911. Some of the prisoners were taken to Fort Smith, Arkansas, where they were tried and condemned by Judge Isaac Parker. The famous "King of the Boomers," Captain David Payne, was twice confined here for illegally attempting to settle on Indian lands. (FSM)

The Marlow brothers (George, Boone, Alfred, Lewellyn or "Epp," and Charles) behind the barracks on the Quadrangle at Fort Sill, Indian Territory in 1885. This was shortly before the arrest and transfer of these Indian Territory outlaws to a Texas jail. Two of the surviving brothers would later become lawmen. They have been the subject of numerous books and movies such as *The Sons of Katie Elder*. (FSM)

or stand. His name was Frederick Remington, and he came from a place called New York to paint pictures of the native people much the same as George Catlin had done over fifty years before.

He was very talented, and I was most impressed by his ability to capture the appearance and feelings of these people on the sketchpads and framed canvas. As others had done before him, he also made extensive notes about his experiences in this area that soon appeared in the magazines and newspapers back east. I often wondered what the light-colored people who lived great distances from this place thought about the native people when they saw the paintings and read the stories about their daily lives.

The next few years were very difficult for the native people. The warrior's tradition was all but lost due to the massive changes they had been forced to endure. However, in 1891 the army took a bold step and reestablished Troop L, Seventh U.S. Cavalry at Fort Sill, a unit consisting solely of native soldiers.

A very dedicated and experienced officer named Captain Hugh L. Scott was placed in command of this experimental unit. He understood better than anyone else the values and customs of the native people and also how this could benefit the army. Captain Scott's knowledge and understanding made it possible for these warriors of the past to hold their heads high and regain their pride from the old days. He often traveled to other army posts as well as to the West Point Military Academy teaching the sign language to army officers so they could better communicate with the native people. Captain Scott later became General Scott, Chief of Staff of the Army.

Ironically, many different birds relayed the story to me that Troop L originally consisted of light-colored soldiers under the command of our old acquaintance, Lieutenant Colonel George A. Custer. In the spring of 1876, Custer and much of his command, including Troop L, were totally destroyed in battle by native warriors at a place called "Little Big Horn" far to the north in Montana. I continue to be amazed that the history of Fort Sill is so far-reaching and so full of connections and unique circumstances!

One of the Kiowa soldiers from Troop L by the name of "I-See-O," also known as "Tah-bone-mah," distinguished himself during a very chaotic and confusing time after 1890 when a religious movement known as the "Ghost Dance" swept across the west. I heard that more than two hundred men, women, and children of the native people were killed at a place called Wounded Knee

Captain Hugh L. Scott was the commander of Troop L, Seventh U.S. Cavalry at Fort Sill, consisting of Kiowa, Comanche, and Apache soldiers, and was also the army's leading expert on sign language. Known by the Indians as "Mor-or-tay-wah," Scott later rose to the rank of general and served in many important capacities for both the army and the U.S. government. (Photographer: George Addison) (FSM)

in South Dakota because of the fear and mistrust the light-colored people had for this movement.

Word of this tragedy quickly spread to Fort Sill as many of the native people in this area were also embracing the Ghost Dance. A similar tragedy as occurred at Wounded Knee was averted here primarily through the efforts of I-See-O and another prominent Kiowa leader named "Ah-pea-tone" or "Wooden Lance." They worked very hard to keep everyone calm. In recognition of his successful efforts, I-See-O was later given the permanent rank of "Senior Duty Sergeant in the U.S. Army," never to be reduced or retired until his death in 1927.

In the early fall of 1894, when my leaves began to turn reddish-orange in color, another group of native people called the Chiricahua and Warm Springs Apache arrived at Fort Sill. They had fought a long war in the desert and mountain country of Arizona until their final surrender in the fall of 1886. They were first sent to Florida as prisoners of war where they became ill and began to die in large numbers. In less than two years they were moved to the humid forested areas of Alabama, but it was not much better there. They liked the sun and were uncomfortable under the tall trees in that region, so they were eventually sent to Fort Sill for a new beginning.

Among their many famous warrior leaders were Geronimo, Nana, Chatto, and Naiche, the son of yet another great warrior known as Cochise. Geronimo or "Goy-ah-kla" (One Who Yawns) was a warrior of great controversy among both the Apaches and the soldiers. He had resisted the army for many years and was both feared and respected by all that came in contact with him. During his time at Fort Sill he attracted a lot of attention, and I frequently saw him with groups of soldiers and civilians alike who were always watching and listening to what he had to say. I even saw him playing baseball one time and when he was hit with a ball on the shin, he let out quite a howl! Some were afraid of what he might do.

I-See-O, Kiowa soldier in Troop L, Seventh U.S. Cavalry and later Sergeant of Scouts, was instrumental in saving many lives during the Ghost Dance activities around Fort Sill in 1890–1891. As a result, he was later awarded the previously unheard-of rank, "Senior Duty Sergeant in the U.S. Army"—never to be reduced or retired. (Photographer: Morris Swett) (FSM)

In the winter of 1909, Geronimo died of pneumonia and his body was placed in the little stone morgue behind the post hospital until burial arrangements could be made. I will never forget hearing the cries and wailing of the Apache women throughout the day following his death until the horse-drawn hearse came to take him to the Apache cemetery for burial. It is most intriguing to me that one hundred years after his death in the winter of 1909, he continues to be the focus of curiosity and controversy.

Another very curious thing happened at Fort Sill in 1894. These wild Apache warriors, who were officially prisoners of war, were also enlisted into the army as soldiers in Troop L, Seventh U.S. Cavalry. They wore uniforms, were paid a salary,

The famous Apache war leader Geronimo relayed his life story to biographer E .M. Barrett (left) and the Apache interpreter Asa Daklugie (right) at Fort Sill in 1906. (Photographer: Edward Bates) (FSM)

and even carried firearms just as other native soldiers did. They also became skilled baseball players along with the other Comanche, Kiowa, and Plains Apache soldiers and they frequently competed against the light-colored soldiers in ball games that were sometimes considered to be mock battles.

According to the grapevine, most of the soldiers left Fort Sill in 1898 to fight in the Spanish-American War in a place called Cuba, and afterward, in another distant place called the Philippines. Only twenty-one soldiers and their families stayed behind to occupy Fort Sill during this period of conflict. I heard that the first officer killed in Cuba was Lieutenant Allyn Capron Jr.,

a cavalry officer from Fort Sill who had joined an elite fighting force known as the "Rough Riders." I had seen Lieutenant Capron riding in the vicinity of the Medicine Bluffs on numerous occasions, and the news of his death came as a shock for both his family and friends who still lived at the fort. By chance, Mrs. Capron was speaking on the telephone with a friend when the official word of her husband's death was announced over the same telephone to the headquarters office. She promptly fainted and fell to the floor. My leaves dropped to the ground about this time!

One of the Apache soldiers by the name of Sam Haozous was a very good friend of Lieutenant Capron, and after hearing of his tragic death in combat, named his next child Allyn Capron Haozous in honor of his friend. However, this child did not survive, and it was several years before Sam had another child, whom he also named Allyn Capron Haozous. This was the first Apache child born in freedom after their prisoner of war status was lifted. As a young adult, Allyn Capron Haozous became better known as Allan Houser, the famous Apache artist whose traditional but stylistic paintings and sculptures were eagerly sought after by museums and collectors throughout the world.

Another very unusual event occurred in 1898 during the conflict in Cuba. The twenty-one soldiers who remained behind when this war first began were very excited one day when rumors spread that Geronimo and more than three hundred Apache prisoners of war were

Eli Coffee ("Hu-wedica" or "Hovah-rith-ka", Coffee Eater/Coffee Drinker), a Comanche soldier in Troop L, Seventh U.S. Cavalry, and also a U.S. Scout under Captain Hugh L. Scott (Photographer: Ogle McCoy) (FSM)

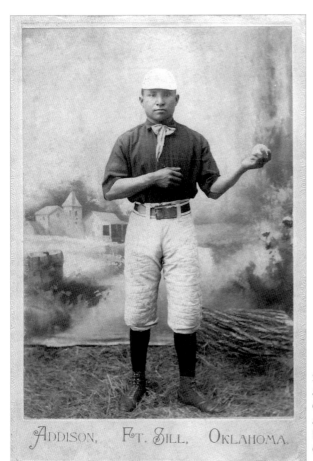

planning to rise up and take over the fort. Lieutenant Beech, the acting commander of the post, was unfamiliar with these native people, and he mistrusted Geronimo very much. Lieutenant Beech sent telegrams to Rush Springs and also to Fort Grant, New Mexico, requesting help since he feared an attack could come at any time. Troop B of the Seventh Cavalry under the command of Lieutenant S. R. H. "Tommy" Tompkins started a forced march from Fort Grant across the Texas

Sam Haozous, Apache POW and Troop L soldier in his baseball uniform at Fort Sill (circa 1896). Sam was the father of the internationally famous Chiricahua Apache artist/sculptor, Allan Capron Houser. Allan was named after Sam's good friend, Lieutenant Allyn Capron, who was the first officer killed in Cuba during the Spanish-American War in 1898. (Photographer: George Addison) (FSM)

The last muster of the inter-tribal military unit, Troop L, Seventh U.S. Cavalry, was photographed at Fort Sill, Oklahoma Territory, on May 31, 1896. The Fort Sill unit was composed solely of Kiowa, Comanche, and Apache soldiers and was the last of the experimental Troop L units in the U.S. Army to stand down in 1897 before converting to U.S. scouts. (FSM)

panhandle to the Indian Territory in an effort to protect the fort from the rumored attack by these native people.

Strangely, a special group of native warriors led by Quanah Parker quickly came to the aid of the army since he did not like the Apaches. Quanah came to the post with his own army of Comanche warriors and offered his services to defend the fort against the Apache until the light-colored soldiers arrived from New Mexico. This was a very puzzling twist of history indeed! Watching this unusual drama unfold was a most intriguing experience for me. It was soon determined that Lieutenant Beech had panicked unnecessarily and there was no truth to the rumors about a possible attack by the Apache. Lieutenant Beech was now in a lot of trouble

with the army, and Lieutenant Tompkins was not amused either.

It was not until 1913 that the Chiricahua and Warm Springs Apache people were officially released as prisoners of war. By their own choice, approximately two-thirds of the people moved to the Mescalero Apache Reservation in New Mexico, and one-third elected to stay in the vicinity of Fort Sill. Hereafter, the latter group was referred to as the "Fort Sill Apache." This was indeed a most unique journey for these native people. Today, many of these native soldiers and their families are buried within the seven cemeteries located on Fort Sill.

The Diary: Coming of Age

By the summer of 1901, more than 29,000 settlers came to Fort Sill to register for homesteads as the so-called "surplus" lands in the Kiowa, Comanche, and Apache country were made available to outsiders. The western half of Indian Territory had become known as Oklahoma Territory in 1890, and Fort Sill was the center of activity in this area. This land opening was among the last of several that permitted the light-colored people to enter and settle on what had been the lands of the native people. However, unlike all other previous land openings, the Kiowa, Comanche, and Apache lands were to be opened by lottery rather than by a land rush involving thousands of people racing into the area at one time.

There were many little camps of tents and wagons to the east and south of the post, and the army was kept very busy trying to maintain some sense of order while they waited to see who would receive the land. Out of this turmoil, I witnessed the birth of a new city called "Lawton" a short distance south of Fort Sill in the summer of 1901. It was named after a very brave soldier, Major General Henry Lawton, who had been killed in the Philippines not long before. Lawton

Photo taken in September 1901 depicting portable buildings being moved in the city of Lawton, established overnight on August 6, 1901, when the Kiowa, Comanche, and Apache lands were officially opened for settlement. Lawton was named after General Henry Lawton, who had served at Fort Sill as a young lieutenant in the 1870s and was killed in the Philippines in 1900. (MGP)

had served at Fort Sill in the 1870s as a lieutenant in charge of the Quartermaster Department, and he was very well liked and respected.

Among the thousands of light-colored people who came to this area after 1901 was a very famous outlaw by the name of Frank James. Frank and his brother Jesse were legends in the world for robbing banks and trains following the Civil War. They had ranged from the far north country of Minnesota to Texas during their unlawful escapades and were known nationwide. Jesse was eventually slain by one of his own gang members, and Frank ultimately was sent to prison.

After a few years and his debt to society having been paid, Frank and his family came to this area around 1907 for a fresh start and to take advantage of the many opportunities available as a result of the land openings and statehood. He purchased a house in the nearby town of Fletcher and stayed a couple of years before returning to Missouri. It was very exciting to see this outlaw legend come and go around Fort Sill for a while.

With the new century came changes in modern warfare as the Twenty-ninth Battery of Artillery was established at Fort Sill in 1902. Over the next few years other groups of artillerymen also arrived and began organizing into provisional fighting units. The loud roar of the big guns was most impressive but also very disruptive at this time. By 1907, the cavalry began leaving, and it appeared that only the temporary or provisional units of artillery and some elements of the Thirteenth Infantry would remain at Fort Sill.

A rather unusual character known as Theodore or "Teddy" Roosevelt visited Fort Sill on numerous occasions. He was a hero of the recent conflict in Cuba, and everyone gathered around him when he spoke. Frequently, he would visit with the prominent Comanche leader Quanah Parker at his ranch about fifteen miles west of here. Quanah's house was known as "Star House" because he painted sixteen stars on the roof, declaring to the world that he outranked any general officer who ever came to visit him.

Teddy Roosevelt often sought Quanah's advice, and they would frequently go hunting together. This former soldier, now a politician, was heavily involved in creating a National Forest Preserve in the nearby Wichita Mountains, and in 1907, he and Frank Rush helped reestablish some of the buffalo that had disappeared from the grassy meadows many years earlier. The gossip on the grapevine was that Colonel Roosevelt soon became President of the United States of America.

The return of the buffalo to the Wichita Mountains attracted a lot of attention in 1907. They were almost all eliminated from the southern plains by 1879 as a result of intensive commercial hunting that was encouraged by the army in an effort to help control the warring tribes at the time. It was a sad time for me when these great herds no longer sought grass, water,

Theodore "Teddy" Roosevelt often visited Fort Sill to hunt and also meet with military and tribal leaders. As President of the United States, he was heavily involved in establishing a forest preserve in the nearby Wichita Mountains as well as the eventual statehood of Oklahoma in 1907. (FSM)

or relief from the hot summer sun beneath my shady branches.

Thirteen buffalo were brought from the New York Zoological Society to begin repopulating the southern plains. These same animals were descended from buffalo that originally came from the plains of northwest Oklahoma many years before. It was a small step forward, but it was nonetheless a very powerful step in the right direction. Many of the native people in the area passed my home on Medicine Bluffs Creek on their way to greet the returning buffalo that had once been their very life's blood. Ironically, the light-colored people gave names to some of these first buffalo, such as "Quanah," "Satanta," and "Geronimo" after the native leaders who had been their former enemies. It was a great day and we all rejoiced! Today, this same herd of buffalo is maintained at approximately six hundred head on the Wichita Mountains Wildlife Refuge located immediately north of Fort Sill.

Surprisingly, there were discussions in 1907 about tearing down the stone buildings that were first erected beginning in 1869, and a very important person came from the United States capital in Washington, D.C., to investigate the matter. The trees planted by Colonel Ranald Mackenzie some thirty-two years earlier passed the word to me that Secretary of War William Howard Taft and Post Trader William Quinette rode in a buggy around the quadrangle and discussed the many important people and incidents involving the history of the old stone buildings.

After hearing the very interesting and significant history of this place, Taft proclaimed the old stone fort should be left alone just as it was. The army would have to move farther west and build another complete post for the artillery. Secretary Taft and President Roosevelt were among the first political leaders to support the preservation of the early history and natural resources of this area. Soon after this visit, Secretary Taft also became the President of the United States of America. These were great people indeed!

I noted on one occasion that the increased settlement of the area led to several divisions and reorganizations of the old Indian Territory. In 1890, the Indian Territory was split into two territories as a result of dividing the land among the native people and the light-colored people. The eastern half continued to be known as Indian Territory, but the western half now was referred to as Oklahoma Territory. Fort Sill's mailing address changed from "I. T." or Indian Territory, to "O. T." or Oklahoma Territory, after 1890. In 1905, there was an attempt to bring both territories into the Union as separate states, with the western half called "Oklahoma" and the eastern half "Sequoyah." However, our old friend President Theodore Roosevelt did not want two separate states and killed the bill. Late in the fall of 1907, the Indian and Oklahoma

Secretary of War, later President, William H. Taft was responsible for saving the original historic buildings at Fort Sill from destruction or severe modification when he visited the post in 1907. (FSM)

A "New Post" was constructed farther west from the original fort and southeast from the Medicine Bluffs in 1909–1911 to better accommodate the new mission of field artillery. Officers' family quarters on the north line are depicted in this photo. (Photographer: Edward Bates) (FSM)

Territories were rejoined to become the state of Oklahoma, and a forty-sixth star was added to the national flag.

During the period of 1909 to 1911, the new artillery post was constructed farther west of the old fort using concrete and stucco as well as some brick instead of stone. The roofs were of red clay tile with iron railings, and the porches, windows, and doors sported arched openings. They tell me this style of architecture is referred to as "Spanish

Mission Revival." Rumor has it there was a lot of graft and corruption involving contractors in the construction of this new fort.

A very honorable man known as Captain David L. Stone assumed the quartermaster position and soon straightened it all out. Captain Stone removed the bad guys and canceled their contracts, saving the government a lot of money in completing the construction. However, some of the corrupt contractors had friends in Washington, D.C., and they complained very

Far Left: Captain Dan T. Moore, former aide and boxing partner to President Theodore Roosevelt, established the first School of Fire for Field Artillery at Fort Sill in 1911. (FSM)

Left: Colonel (later Major General) William J. Snow was responsible for reviving the faltering School of Fire for Field Artillery at Fort Sill in 1917. The post commander at that time was an infantryman who had ordered the previous commandant for the artillery school off the post. (FSM)

loudly, whereupon the War Department ordered Captain Stone to pay a large fine for not following proper contracting procedures.

But in the tradition of the strongest oak tree in the forest, Captain Stone stood firm against this assault and said, if anything, the War Department owed him money, and he would take Fort Sill as payment if they persisted with their accusations. Fearing a major scandal, everyone calmed down and backed off. Captain Stone was truly a committed individual and he survived this political pressure, continuing to serve in the army until his retirement as a major general at Fort Lewis, Washington.

Sometime around 1910, the peace and quiet of the fort was disturbed when the first "horseless carriage" appeared on the scene. Making a very irritating noise and belching foul-smelling smoke behind it, the little carriage with driver moved rapidly along the Fort Sill roads leaving many frightened horses in its wake. It was a sight to behold, and everyone was very excited! It was my

sincerest wish at the time, however, that I would never see another one like it.

In 1911, I also witnessed the establishment at Fort Sill of the new School of Fire for Field Artillery by Captain Dan T. Moore. Captain Moore had been an aide and boxing partner for President Roosevelt, and he was very quick on his feet. Artillery training at Fort Sill was greatly improved through his tireless efforts. In addition, units of the Fifth Artillery began deploying to the Mexican border from 1912 to 1915 because there were serious concerns about revolutionary armies and the ever-present outlaws crossing the Rio Grande River into this country.

At the same time there were other unusual activities happening in the nearby mountains and valleys to the north of Medicine Bluffs Creek. Strangely enough, groups of soldiers, native people, and others were engaged in role-playing for cameras that produced moving pictures on film. These were later known as "movies" or "motion pictures." This activity was apparently driven by romantic feelings

The Fifth Field Artillery Battalion with the horse-drawn, Model 1902, three-inch gun and limber crossing Medicine Bluffs Creek in 1913 (Photographer: Edward Bates) (FSM)

An early five-ton Holt tractor pulling artillery on the west range of Fort Sill (circa 1919). This "motorized artillery," painted in dazzle camouflage, signaled the end of the horse-drawn tradition. The Holt Tractor Company would later become the Caterpillar Tractor Company. (Photographer: Edward Bates) (FSM)

of nostalgia and adventure based on some of the very history I had personally witnessed through the years. The world was changing, and the people wanted to preserve and relive the glories of their past before they were lost. The ready availability of soldiers, native people, and buffalo in the picturesque setting of the Wichita Mountains provided all the ingredients that were needed for this new adventure.

The first silent movies I witnessed being produced were called *The Bank Robbery* and *The Wolf Hunt* in 1908. Our old friends Quanah Parker and Teddy Roosevelt were involved in these projects as well as Deputy U.S. Marshal Jack Abernathy. These were followed in 1913 by other exciting movies produced by the famous scout and hunter Buffalo Bill Cody using local native people and soldiers from the Fifth Artillery.

In the fall of 1914, I witnessed the filming of another unusual movie, called *Sign of the Smoke* by the Geronimo Film Company, featuring more than one hundred Comanche and Kiowa people, twenty cowboys from both Texas and Oklahoma, men and women from the famous 101 Ranch Wild West Show in northern Oklahoma, and a herd of 125 buffalo.

Beginning in 1915, prominent western lawmen, Deputy U.S. Marshals Bill Tilghman and Chris Madsen, organized the Eagle Film Company so they could produce silent movies to counteract similar adventure epochs featuring Al Jennings, a lawyer and second-rate outlaw who had served time in prison. The resulting movies such as *The Passing of the Oklahoma Outlaws* reflected the lawless days of the Indian and Oklahoma Territories.

This was followed in 1919 by another silent movie called *Daughter of the Dawn*, featuring a

Village scene from the 1919 silent movie, *Daughter of the Dawn*, filmed on Fort Sill and in the nearby Wichita Mountains. The all-native cast was led by the Kiowa warrior Hunting Horse, who is seen here in council with other Kiowa and Comanche warriors/actors. (Photographer: Edward Bates) (FSM)

cast composed solely of native people including White Parker and Wanada Parker, the son and daughter of the famous Comanche war chief, Quanah Parker. Quanah's family also appeared in *Sign of the Smoke*, completed five years earlier. It was interesting to note that the army was heavily involved in the production of these early movies. This odd behavior, demonstrated by such a variety of characters who had a few years earlier opposed each other on the battlefield, was very entertaining for the many squirrels and birds perched among my branches.

Many years later, I was most impressed to observe certain soldiers while serving at Fort Sill who would become giants in the motion picture industry. A sergeant by the name of Victor Fleming routinely conducted experiments in filming explosions on the Fort Sill ranges in the early 1920s, and after leaving the army, he studied at the New York Film Academy and eventually ended up in a place called Hollywood, California.

Fleming directed two very important movies that became classics in American history and won many prestigious honors known as Academy Awards or Oscars in 1939, *Gone with the Wind* and *The Wizard of Oz*.

I also remember a soldier by the name of Louis L'Amour, who served as a boxing instructor at Fort Sill around 1943. Later, I was fascinated to learn that he became famous for writing western novels, many of which were made into very successful movies about cowboys, outlaws, soldiers, and native people. His early experiences and exposure to the history around Fort Sill, and Oklahoma in general, contributed greatly to his success in writing books that were made into western movies.

Another group of special soldiers came to Fort Sill in 1913 that looked like all the others yet acted somewhat differently. Although there had been infantry units at Fort Sill from the beginning, this new group made a special effort to establish the "School of Musketry" or the "School of Arms" as they began intensive training with rifles and machine guns. They always seemed to be marching around with their rifles and digging holes and trenches in the dirt before rushing forth to another location, only to repeat this strange behavior again and again. I was puzzled by their antics!

When the School of Musketry was transferred from Fort Sill to Fort Benning, Georgia, in 1918 to become the new U.S. Army Infantry School, a historical pageant was performed in their honor along Medicine Bluffs Creek, a short distance east of my home. The artillery soldiers wanted to say farewell to the infantry soldiers by celebrating the "old army" and the "new army" as of that time. Many hundreds of soldiers gathered on the steep slope behind the old hospital to witness the event

taking place in the valley below.

A small log house surrounded by a log wall was constructed in the center of the little valley along the creek, and various activities were featured on either side. Artillery weapons were situated on the east side of the little fort to represent the latest technology of the "new army," while a reenactment of the old days or the "old army" was to take place on the opposite side of the log structure. The reenactment was partially a mock battle symbolizing an attack on the fort by the native people using the local Comanche, Kiowa, and Apache warriors. Many of these warriors were veterans of combat against the soldiers during the Red River War, and memories of the old days were still fresh in their minds.

The pageant story had the native people attacking the little fort only to be repelled by the

INFANTRY ON HIKE
CAMP DONIPHAN, OKLA.   43.

Although infantry units had been at Fort Sill since the beginning, the School of Musketry was the first organized training for the soldiers in a school concept beginning in 1913. The school was relocated to Fort Benning, Georgia, in 1918. This 1917 view depicts infantry soldiers associated with Camp Doniphan, a training camp for the Missouri and Kansas National Guard that was located on Fort Sill during World War I. (FSM)

Scene from the farewell pageant presented in 1918 by the Field Artillery School of Fire for the School of Musketry before they departed Fort Sill to become the new Infantry School at Fort Benning, Georgia. The little log palisade and cabin represented the "Old West" when Fort Sill was first established. The event was complete with an attack by Indians, a ride for help, and the army coming to the rescue. The latest artillery weapons were also on display. The pageant occurred on Medicine Bluffs Creek immediately behind the old hospital. (FSM)

horse-mounted artillery soldiers who were actually impersonating the cavalry. "Wo-haw" or "Beef," one of the old Kiowa warriors and a veteran of many battles, was suspicious of the army and felt this would be the last true fight to the death. He could not be convinced that everyone would be firing blank ammunition and that it was simply a reenactment of the old days. I, too, had great concerns about the coming battle and its effect on the participants.

As the attack commenced, the smoke from the blank ammunition quickly covered the battlefield, and visibility was severely limited. The mounted soldiers soon came to the aid of the little log fort and rousted the attacking native warriors as planned. However, there was so much gun smoke over the little valley that it took a while to clear away so the audience, sitting on the sloping hillside and waiting anxiously with bated breath, could see what had happened.

Most of the warriors had retreated to the

outer edge of the battle site, but lying on the ground near the little log fort was the body of "Wo-haw." Everyone rushed to his aid and found that he was unconscious and bleeding from a head wound. It was soon determined that he had been knocked to the ground by a soldier's horse, hitting his head on a tree stump in the process. To his dying day, "Wo-haw" could not be convinced that the army was not using live ammunition, and he often recounted how he had fought in the last great battle with the soldiers at Fort Sill in 1918. The many ironies depicted in these movies and pageants during this time were most intriguing, but also very entertaining for the trees and animals of the forest along Medicine Bluffs Creek.

It was in 1915 that I noticed the First Aero Squadron buzzing around overhead in their new flying machines. Some large wooden crates were brought to the parade ground of the old fort a few days earlier where the little flying machines were unpacked and assembled, then walked down the hill to be flown for the first time. This was the first aviation unit in the American military, and the pilots, I am told, were trained by someone called the Wright brothers. It was truly a remarkable sight, and I do not understand it even today. The little flying machines, with their double wings and single propeller in front, were always zipping here and there taking photographs and directing artillery fire on targets.

Later that year when the unit left Fort Sill to conduct additional training at Fort Sam Houston, Texas, their journey became the first squadron flight in American aviation history. I was amazed that it took only a week for them to reach Fort Sam Houston near San Antonio. It was later revealed to me that while at Fort Sill they produced the first aerial mosaic photographs ever taken in history.

The large sausage-like balloons that followed these little winged aircraft a short time later were even more ominous in their size and silence. The birds that rested on my branches would suddenly flutter skyward when these large behemoths loomed overhead. We watched as these gigantic balloons of the "First Balloon Corps" crossed the sky ever so slowly, and the birds would chirp loudly while mocking their apparent clumsiness.

On one occasion in 1918, I witnessed a horrible scene when one of these balloons exploded on the ground. It had been filled with the very dangerous hydrogen gas, allowing it to float effortlessly above the landscape but at great risk, since it was also quite flammable. The loud shock waves of the explosion and the resulting fireball could easily be seen and felt from my upper branches, causing many squirrels to fall to the ground. I understand that six soldiers were killed in this explosion and many others were badly burned.

With the establishment in 1917 of Henry Post Army Airfield on the large pasture just south of the stone buildings, many different kinds of aircraft came to this area for testing and training. The designation of Fort Sill as an aviation center for the army was due to the efforts of Secretary of War Patrick Hurley, a great hero and aviation enthusiast who was also native-born in the Indian Territory. Many other famous aviation celebrities such as Wiley Post and Charles Lindbergh visited this place over the years. Lindbergh actually

A squadron of Curtis JN-4 "Jenny" aeroplanes flying in formation over Fort Sill (circa 1917–20). The First Aero Squadron flew Curtis JN-2 aircrafts at Fort Sill in 1915 while training in artillery observation, aerial photography, and mapping. During this training, they produced the first aerial mosaic photos in the world, and their departing flight from Fort Sill to Fort Sam Houston, Texas, was the first squadron flight in American aviation history. (FSM)

Henry Post Army Airfield, established in 1917, is seen here with Curtis JN-4 "Jenny" aeroplanes on the ground, and a "sausage" observation balloon with gondola basket flying overhead (circa 1918–1920). Wiley Post, the world-famous aviator, began his career as a construction worker on this airfield. (FSM)

The explosion of a hydrogen-filled balloon on Henry Post Army Airfield at Fort Sill in 1918 caused the death of six soldiers and severe injuries to many others. This incident predated that of the Hindenburg in 1938, which resulted from the same problem of static electricity igniting a very volatile gas. This scene was published in many national magazines of the day such as *Mechanix Illustrated* and *National Geographic*. (FSM)

flew over the great waters to the east by himself. Later still, Wiley Post, who in 1917 had helped construct the airfield, succeeded in flying around the entire world. This was truly amazing!

By 1916, many of the soldiers had left the

Colonel Charles A. Lindbergh with Major (later Lieutenant General) Lewis E. Brereton at Fort Sill on February 23, 1929. Following his famous trans-Atlantic flight to Paris, France, Lindbergh toured the United States to promote aviation. (Photographer: Morris Swett) (FSM)

post to participate in the "Punitive Expedition" that marched deep into northern Mexico under the command of General John J. Pershing. I heard that this campaign attracted a lot of attention, but little of significance was actually accomplished. However, they were able to test many of the new weapons and equipment that would soon prove useful to the soldiers when they became involved with the "Great War" across the big waters in Europe. The Great War, otherwise known as World War I, caused a tremendous flurry of activity around Fort Sill.

The School of Fire for Field Artillery that had been organized and established in 1911 had fallen on hard times and was later shut down when the commander of the post, who happened to be an infantryman, ordered the artillery school commander off the post. It was left to Colonel William J. Snow to restart the school in 1917 so the soldiers could again receive the intensive artillery training they needed to participate in this new conflict in Europe. I personally felt the two commanders were acting a little silly and they should have fought it out somewhere along the creek where I could watch.

With this new conflict came new technology, some of it from across the great waters to the east. The army of the French nation developed a secret artillery weapon in 1897 and had managed to restrict its manufacture from any other country. It was the 75-mm Gun, Model 1897, and it had a special recoil system that eliminated problems of realignment on the target after firing each round and thus could be reloaded and fired faster and more accurately. The French army brought this weapon to Fort Sill in 1917 and used it in training U.S. soldiers for the first time.

Many other groups of soldiers arrived at Fort Sill during this time, and training activities increased everywhere. A large training camp named Camp Doniphan was established in 1917 immediately west of the fort to provide training for the Missouri and Kansas National Guard troops. One of the

Lieutenant (later Captain) Harry S. Truman served in the 129th Infantry Division at Camp Doniphan on Fort Sill in 1917 before shipping out for France during World War I. Many of the letters to his wife that were published in his book *Dear Bess* were written from Fort Sill. Truman later became U.S. President. (FSM)

parades of soldiers along with their trucks, tanks, artillery, and airplanes marched down the streets of Lawton. The community greeted them warmly, and everyone was happy that the long war was finally over. There were also many captured enemy artillery weapons brought home after the war and they were proudly displayed as trophies around the old guardhouse and the Liberty Theatre just a short distance southwest of my home on the creek.

In 1918, I was 154 years old, and although in my middle age, I was still full of vim and vigor. My branches were continuing to extend outward, and my crown kept reaching skyward. I was among the largest trees in the forest, and I felt invincible. However, the twentieth century was still young, and there would be many challenges for me to face in the coming years. The following decades of the 1920s and 1930s were also a time of recovery and reorientation for the army.

After a few years, I noticed that someone was setting fire to a large number of buildings on the post, and the people became very concerned about where the next fires might occur. The problem was so severe that all new construction was halted until the culprits could be caught and punished. Following an extended period of chaos caused by the arson, it was determined that the bad people worked in the fire department and in the military police. They were stealing anything valuable during the confusion while fighting the fires. Undercover police finally caught them, and they were soon sent to prison in Fort Leavenworth, Kansas. Afterward, a surge of new construction took place all over the post beginning in 1934–1935.

A welcome distraction from this horrible situation occurred in the early 1930s. I vividly recall a famous cowboy-entertainer by the name of Will Rogers, who often performed for the soldiers in the nearby Liberty Theatre, coming to Fort Sill. The theatre was only a stone's throw from my home on Medicine Bluffs Creek, and I could easily see everything that occurred there.

soldiers who trained at Camp Doniphan was Lieutenant Harry S. Truman. I observed him being promoted to captain before leaving Fort Sill for the battlefields of France. Many people said that he was very outspoken and action-oriented. One day I heard the blue jay birds say that he later became President of the United States. It was fascinating to see these great men rise to such heights and become so important in the people's world.

After the Great War concluded in late 1918, I watched as the little huts and tents of Camp Doniphan were torn down and the troops returned home. It was a time of great celebration and

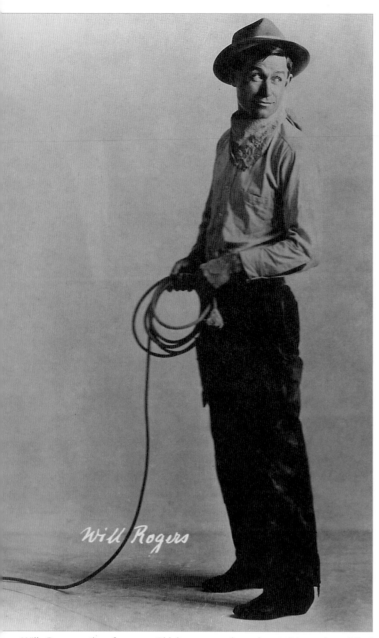

Will Rogers, the famous Oklahoma cowboy, humorist, and political commentator, came to Fort Sill frequently during the early 1930s. Rogers frequently competed on the polo field and also entertained the troops in the Liberty Theatre approximately two hundred yards from the Silent Witness bur oak tree. (AUTH)

Will Rogers was a native son of Oklahoma, descended from both the "Ani-yun-wiya" or Cherokee Nation and also the light-colored people. He was world-renowned for his sense of humor and political wit. During his monthly visits to Fort Sill, he often hung around the fire department and listened to gossip about other people on the post. On Saturday evenings, he would present programs to large audiences of soldiers in the theater building and tell jokes based on this gossip while twirling his rope in loops around his feet and head. I could easily hear the continuous laughter from his jokes across the little valley, and it was all I could do to keep from breaking my branches or accidentally dropping my acorns while chuckling so hard.

There were other notable cowboy entertainers who followed Will Rogers to Fort Sill over the years. I remember a young cowboy by the name of Gene Autry, who frequently came here to entertain the soldiers. Although born in Tioga, Texas, as a small child he had moved with his family to southern Oklahoma where he matured to adulthood. As a young man, Gene often sang and played the guitar while working as a railroad telegrapher in the Ravia depot.

He first came to the attention of Will Rogers in 1928, and he would ultimately have a major impact in movies as well as in the fields of music and baseball. I was very proud of Gene when he joined the Army Air Corps in 1942, and he would often come to Fort Sill to sing his melodies for the troops. He soon married a girl from the nearby town of Duncan, Oklahoma, by the name of Vera Spivey, and they enjoyed many years of wedded bliss. That name is awfully familiar to me for some reason!

The arrival of the 1940s also brought a second war of worldwide proportions. The first "Great War" did not completely eliminate some of the problems in Europe, and it became necessary to go back again. In addition, the soldiers were also engaged in conflict with a far-off Asian country called Japan. Many soldiers received basic and specialized artillery training at Fort Sill before leaving for these distant places. Some did not return home at all.

In the winter of 1941, I heard rumors of another unusual group of native people joining the army. In addition to many other native people recruited from my area, seventeen Comanche warriors were also selected for special communications training by the army. I had witnessed many of the warrior

Snow Hall, the 1917 headquarters for the Field Artillery School, was named after MG William J. Snow. It was destroyed on August 8, 1929, by arsonists who were responsible for burning many other buildings on Fort Sill in order to loot them during the confusion. (Photographer: Morris Swett) (FSM)

The Liberty Theatre was an important place for entertaining the troops in the post–World War I period. This 1923 image shows one of the German artillery war trophies placed in front of the building following the war. The Liberty Theatre was destroyed by an arsonist in 1929. (Photographer: Morris Swett) (FSM)

ancestors of these same men fighting against the army around Fort Sill seventy-five years earlier. Now they were receiving training so they could use their native language and serve as "code-talkers" to prevent the enemy from understanding critical communications between different army units.

I heard that fourteen of them actually saw combat against the Germans across the great waters to the east, and they performed magnificently. The enemy never understood their language code, and they contributed to the success of numerous battles. It was also rumored that some Kiowa warriors from this area served as "code-talkers" during this war although they had not received special training for this purpose. We were glad to see them all return home safely after the war.

Among the many heroes of this new war was a native of the "Muscogee" or Creek Nation, who began and ended his military career at Fort Sill. As a young soldier, Lieutenant Ernest Childers went on to defend his country above and beyond the call of duty in Europe, and his bravery in combat was appropriately recognized when he was awarded the Medal of Honor. I never cease to be impressed with these strange twists of fate involving the native soldiers—their ancestors fought against the army, but the descendants of these warriors sacrificed and fought valiantly with the army in later years to protect their homeland.

A very symbolic event occurred on the parade ground of the old stone fort in 1942. I watched with solemn respect as the last horse-drawn artillery unit finally bowed to the dominance of the motorized artillery and officially stood down during special ceremonies. The horse had played a major role in the history of the Fort Sill area since the very beginning.

For hundreds of years, the horse, along with the buffalo, had been the cultural center of the native people in this area. I had often seen herds of wild horses grazing peacefully in the nearby valleys, and at other times, I watched excitedly as the warriors gave chase with ropes to capture

them. Stealing horses was also a driving force for the native warriors, who regularly journeyed south to Texas and Mexico each year for this purpose. The horse was so important that it became a primary indicator of wealth and power for these people.

Likewise, the cavalry depended heavily on the well-trained horse to carry them into combat and journey over great distances to explore, engage their enemies, or establish new forts. Just as with the native warriors, the horse was an extension of the cavalryman's own body and personality, often becoming so closely merged that they could not be easily separated. In addition to the oxen and

Lieutenant Ernest Childers, a member of the Muscogee or Creek Nation, was called to active duty as a member of the Forty-fifth Infantry Division (Oklahoma National Guard) at the beginning of World War II and completed his basic training at Fort Sill. Lieutenant Childers was awarded the Medal of Honor for bravery above and beyond the call of duty during combat in Europe. Ernest Childers later retired with honors at Fort Sill. (45TH IDM)

mules, horses were also used for pulling wagons loaded with supplies, heavy freight, or sleds stacked high with building stone and lumber for construction of the buildings of the fort.

Since the early nineteenth century, horses had drawn the army's artillery to permit rapid movement on the battlefield. Many thousands of horses had been killed during the numerous wars and conflicts over time, and the replacement and training of these horses was a very big part of the army's normal activities. Even as the first machine-driven vehicles began to pull the artillery at Fort Sill around 1917, the horse remained well entrenched in the army culture.

The animals and trees of the forest often witnessed special events involving horses at Fort Sill from the very beginning. At certain times of the year, such as July Fourth celebrations, racing horses for money or prizes was a favorite pastime. Normally, only officers could afford to own and care for these prized animals, and they were frequently the object of heavy gambling.

As the new mechanized world began to displace the function of the horse, there were those individuals who refused to accept the inevitable and, instead, developed new recreational or training needs for the horse. Some of these activities included training the horses to race around a field jumping over fences, ditches, and little hills of stone and dirt. During the 1920s and 1930s, soldiers regularly rode their horses in this fashion in a little valley later referred to as Rucker Park, a short distance down the creek from me. It looked very tiring for the horses, but the training paid off with international recognition when, in 1938, they were awarded special trophies in Mexico City by the National Association of Equestrians of Mexico. I was very proud of them.

Other horse activities at this time included a game called "polo," which consisted of riders swinging long-handled hammers while guiding their horses back and forth across a long open field in pursuit of a small ball. It took great skill to chase that little ball across the field and hit

AIR VIEW OF THE 45 TH DIVISION
FORT SILL OKLA
POST STUDIO

The original training area used by the Oklahoma and Texas National Guard in the 1920s–1930s was renovated at the beginning of World War II as a new training center for the army. This view to the east includes the circular "Artillery Bowl" built in 1939 where the famous western author Louis L'Amour taught boxing in 1943. (Photographer: Post Studio) (FSM)

it at full gallop, causing it to go in the desired direction. It reminded me of the baseball games I had witnessed many years before, but it seemed more chaotic and disorganized. My old friend Will Rogers often came to play this game at Fort Sill during those days.

Still another form of horse activity we often witnessed was called "The Artillery Hunt." It involved the soldiers dressing up in red coats with funny, baggy pants, tall boots, and a black helmet. These riders rode in a different fashion than others I had routinely seen in the past. It was both comical and graceful at the same time. They would gather in groups before starting out into the forested hills at a slow pace. A rather large wagon, known as the "Talley Ho" wagon, was loaded with spectators, and they would follow the mounted riders wherever they went. A pack of dogs always preceded the riders, and their endless barking and howling was particularly irritating to the trees and animals of the forest. As soon as someone spotted a wandering fox, a designated rider would blow a brass horn, and the chase was on.

Suddenly, the riders were at full gallop racing through the woods, jumping over fences, and weaving between the trees and through the creeks in pursuit of the poor fox. The barking and howling increased at this point, and my leaves shivered at the noise. After the hunters chased the fox for a period of time, the hunt came to an end with or without the fox, and everyone settled down again.

I never really understood some of these games the soldiers played, although I realized it took skill and expertise to manage the horses under these unusual circumstances. The off-duty soldiers were regularly engaged in these activities over many years, but they never again reached their peak as during the time before the second Great War began. The 1942 ceremony marking the last horse-drawn artillery unit standing down at Fort Sill was a salute to the role the horse played in the history of the army.

I believe it was around 1943 that I first noticed a large camp of soldiers confined to an area south of the Medicine Bluffs. Their barracks complex was surrounded by a high barbed-wire fence, and they could not come and go as they pleased. These soldiers dressed differently and had the large white letters "PW" painted on their backs.

The World War II German POW Camp at Fort Sill was located south of Randolph Road and the Medicine Bluffs during 1943–1945. Soldiers from Rommel's "Afrika Corps" captured in North Africa lived in this camp. Many of them worked in the power plant rebuilding electrical motors while living at Fort Sill. When the war ended, they were transferred to England where they managed ammunition in support of the British during the Mau-Mau conflict in Africa before eventually returning to Germany. (FSM)

I learned from the blackbirds that these people were not Americans but German and Italian prisoners of war captured in a far-off place called North Africa. They seemed peaceful enough, and I never heard of any real problems with them. By the end of this conflict, they were taken away and eventually returned to their homeland across the great waters to the east.

Sometime later, I also became aware of a second nearby fenced-off area where other prisoners were confined. These men, women, and children were different in their appearance and mannerisms. It was becoming clear to me that the people around Fort Sill were as varied in their appearance and habits as some of the trees in the forest.

A red-tailed hawk landed on one of my upper branches one day and told me that while soaring in the vicinity he had heard this peculiar area referred to as the Japanese Internment Camp. These people did not look like any soldiers I had seen before, and apparently the light-colored soldiers regarded them with great suspicion because of their resemblance to enemy soldiers across the great waters to the west. I heard that most of them came from a place far to the south called the Panama Canal. After a year or so, they also left Fort Sill.

One day I heard the grapevine say there was a new and very powerful force in the world that involved "atomic energy." Some of the stories I have heard about the weapons developed during this "Nuclear Age," as it came to be called, were almost impossible to believe. The use of these very powerful weapons in Japan apparently killed many thousands of the enemy people resulting in a final conclusion to this second Great War, also known as World War II.

After the war ended and many of the soldiers returned home, the post continued to expand with new buildings occupying more land over time. To my surprise, a few years later around 1951, another major conflict erupted in a place called Korea, and once again the post was bustling with activity as soldiers prepared for combat in

Soldiers from XI Corps Artillery fire an eight-inch Howitzer on pockets of Japanese soldiers at Ipo Dam Hill, Luzon, Philippine Islands, May 28, 1945. The name of this howitzer is "Comanche," as seen painted on the tube near the muzzle. (FSM)

yet another distant war. I did not understand the causes of this conflict, but everyone took it very seriously nonetheless.

Soldiers soon gathered at Fort Sill and began intensive training with artillery, including the new atomic cannons. Twenty of these big 280-mm guns were produced, and they, along with their crews, were eventually deployed in various parts of the world where tensions were running high. The mere threat of this weapon was an important consideration in bringing about a truce in the Korean Conflict. In the spring of 1953, two of these same big guns and their crews under the command of Colonel (later Lieutenant General) Benton E. Spivy, left Fort Sill to test fire an atomic projectile in the desert near Frenchmen's Flats, Nevada. This was the first and only time in American history such an event had occurred. Only one of the weapons was fired, and when it returned to Fort Sill a few months later, I was intrigued to learn this single big gun would hereafter be named "Atomic Annie." I wonder if Colonel Spivy was related to my Interpreter friend from the museum. I heard the colonel say once that he had shortened the spelling of his last name so it would be easier to fill in the blanks on the army's forms. Interesting!

The development and use of atomic weapons continued for many decades after the Korean Conflict, and there was considerable tension in the world related to these weapons. I often heard this extended period of tension referred to as the "Cold War" and it was obvious that many of the people in these United States were very concerned about the survival of their country. I could sense it at Fort Sill, and I, too, became very worried about the future.

"Atomic Annie," the M65, 280-mm Gun with Fort Sill crew, fires a nuclear projectile at Frenchmen's Flats, Nevada, on May 25, 1953. The 15-kiloton projectile fired this day was equal to the atomic bomb dropped on Hiroshima, Japan, in World War II. This weapon is now on display at Fort Sill. (Photographer: Jack Cannon) (FSM)

The Diary: A Time of Reflection

As the years passed ever so quickly and the soldiers continued to train at Fort Sill, I frequently witnessed them passing by on their way to and from the ranges, honing their skills in case they were again called upon to defend their country. I watched as they were sent to far-off places called Vietnam, Bosnia, Kosovo, Iraq, and Afghanistan, and again, there was great rejoicing upon their return. There would undoubtedly be more conflicts in the world, and these soldiers were certainly well prepared and highly motivated to do their duty. I could only wish them well in their efforts.

It was also interesting to note that during these conflicts many individual artillery weapons and aircraft used by the army were given names such as "Comanche," "Kiowa," and "Apache," apparently out of respect for their former enemies or the history connected with them. The native warriors of these respective nations were now merged into the army that had been their enemy in the past. Now they were truly an "Army of One."

Interest in preserving the history of Fort Sill and Field Artillery had been developing ever since World War I, and in 1935, a museum was finally established in the old guardhouse just southwest of the complex of stone buildings. The choice of this building for such a worthy cause was not by chance but by design, as a lot of history had occurred here since its construction in 1872. Many famous soldiers, native people, outlaws, and other colorful individuals had been associated with this building, and it seemed like the perfect place to house the historical artifacts that had been gathered.

In the beginning, a lot of attention was focused on this project, and two officers were chosen to address the mission. Captain Harry Larter became the first curator, and as he began organizing the

First Sergeant Pascal C. Poolaw, a member of the Kiowa Nation, was a combat veteran of World War II, Korea, and three tours of Vietnam. Following his second tour in Vietnam, he worked in the Fort Sill Museum before returning to active duty in 1967. He was killed in action in Vietnam that same year. Poolaw received four Silver Stars, five Bronze Stars, and three Purple Hearts among other awards during his career. (FSM)

The new FA School Administration Building was constructed of masonry in 1935 to replace the wood-framed Snow Hall building that had burned in 1929. In 1958, this building became the new Post Headquarters (McNair Hall), and a new administration building (the second Snow Hall) was constructed for the FA School a short distance down the hill. (Photographer: Post Studio) (FSM)

new museum, Captain Wilbur Nye assembled available information to write the history of Fort Sill. Both objectives were soon achieved, and there was much celebration at the time.

However, by 1964, it became apparent that the museum was losing its support, and to my surprise a face from the past intervened and lent his powerful influence to regenerate the interest and support. Harry S. Truman, former artillery officer at Fort Sill who later became President of the United States, contacted the post commander and expressed his concern about preserving Fort Sill's history and inquired why they were not taking better care of the museum's valuable collections. I observed that it was not long before new resources were made available to the museum, and major improvements soon followed.

In 1969, the post celebrated its one-hundredth anniversary, and the museum was heavily involved in the activities. The museum's role continued to expand over the years to include protecting the original stone buildings and also the

significant sites associated with the native people. The original post headquarters building eventually became the museum headquarters, while the museum assumed a major role as the "institutional memory" of Fort Sill. Now the museum curator and staff developed plans and made important decisions about preserving and interpreting the history of Fort Sill from this vantage point.

In the early winter of 2004, one of those curious twists in history occurred involving both the original and the current post headquarters buildings at Fort Sill and briefly tying the past and the present together in a most unusual manner. I had witnessed the construction of the original post headquarters building in 1870 to serve as the center of operations for the army commanders in planning and implementing its many important activities. I had also observed many famous generals and native warrior leaders while they experienced both failures and successes in this modest stone building located in the center of the south line of buildings on the quadrangle.

It was here that the first telephone had been installed connecting the Indian Territory to the rest of the nation in 1879, and the army first received important communications pertaining to statehood for Oklahoma in 1907 and declarations of war and peace by the nation. It was also here that surrenders and/or paroles of prominent native warriors had occurred during and after the Red River War. Court-martial proceedings convened in this building routinely determined the fates of soldiers who had broken the rules. Detailed plans and decisions were also made here regarding the commitment of troops during the Indian Wars in the southern plains and in the Spanish-American War.

Because of the change in mission to artillery and the corresponding expansion of Fort Sill in the early twentieth century, I observed the official headquarters being relocated to the new post farther west a mile or so in 1911, leaving the former headquarters to assume a lesser function. To my surprise, in 1958 the post headquarters was moved yet a third time to the Administration Building for the Field Artillery School that had been built in 1935 (currently known as McNair Hall). The official flag pole and flag had to be relocated each time the headquarters moved. Since that time, major planning and decision-making for the entire post have taken place in this most recent headquarters building.

On one very unusual day in the fall of 2004, a bomb threat was received by telephone at the "Emergency Operations Center" in the headquarters basement, and the entire three-story building and basement had to be evacuated immediately. I was told by several excited birds that shortly after the bomb threat was received, word also came that the Fort Sill National Bank at the PX had been robbed on the east side of the post, and the culprits were attempting to escape with their ill-gotten gains.

It was very exciting to see several hundred people quickly moving from the contemporary headquarters building to the old parade ground of the 1870 fort approximately one hundred yards to the east. Here they stood in the open grassy area facing west toward the more modern three-story headquarters building, waiting with tense anticipation for a potential explosion that might occur at any moment. The museum office in the original 1870 headquarters was immediately commandeered by the "Emergency Operations Center," including the commanding general and staff, military police, and public affairs people. All museum activities ceased, and my Interpreter friend and his staff provided basic support or otherwise stood by and watched as the fast-paced action swirled all around them during the rest of the afternoon.

Emergency telephone and radio communications were quickly set up, and the large table in the museum conference room was covered with maps and other documents for strategic planning to regain control over the present emergency. The public affairs people were controlling all communications to the outside world in an effort to avoid panic or misinformation being released to the public. The law enforcement people were busy coordinating the police units all over the post as well as with state and local law enforcement agencies to gather information and hopefully capture these modern-day outlaws.

I watched with intrigue as many police vehicles raced here and there in anticipation of encountering these bad people at various destinations. The flashing lights and screaming sirens of these vehicles caused me to cringe as they passed by, but the overall atmosphere in the historic headquarters was reflective of a wartime battle in progress with everyone reacting in an orderly but emergency fashion to control rapidly changing events.

The past and the present were colliding head-on in this time and place. It was an experience straight out of the distant past that could easily be compared with similar circumstances from the late nineteenth century when the army would have planned the movement of combat troops against the native people or in pursuit of the outlaws that were not uncommon during that same period. However, by the end of the afternoon it was obvious the confusion resulting from the bomb

Fort Sill continues to be an active deployment center for soldiers to protect the national interests all over the world. This is a typical view of soldiers on patrol in Afghanistan. (DA)

threat in the modern headquarters had its desired effect, and the bank robbers escaped in spite of the army's elaborate efforts to the contrary.

But for a brief moment in time, the clock had been turned back, and nineteenth-century history had inserted itself into the present through a window from the past—a phenomenon that I have witnessed many times. The historic headquarters building had once again served its original purpose after almost ninety years, and although the battle was unsuccessful, much was learned from the process. The irony of the museum's presence and involvement in this contemporary drama would not be lost to me, or to history.

Over the years, a new ball field was established just a stone's throw from where my roots are embedded. I was totally surprised to learn that the soldiers played yet another game that involved striking a ball with some sort of a club. They called it "golf." Amazingly, it seemed the objective was to make the little ball fly through the air before rolling into a small hole in the ground. I never understood why it was so important to make those balls roll into the holes, but I really enjoyed the extra water they lavishly sprayed on the surrounding areas of green grass during the hot summer weather. Fortunately, a cluster of trees was left in place surrounding my magnificent trunk that would protect me from the wayward golf balls as well as the strong winds. These surrounding trees were my friends and relatives,

and they were a comfort to me as I grew older.

One day, my longtime friend and Interpreter from the museum came by to measure me for the historical records. Although it tickled a little bit, I suffered no damage from his efforts. I had grown large in girth and height over the years and now measured sixteen feet around my trunk with some of my lower limbs actually measuring nine feet around their base. However, as I approach my twilight years, the strong winds have begun taking their toll. Not long ago, I lost some of my lower limbs, and my once magnificent spread is now less than it was. My scars from encounters long ago continue to heal over and are less noticeable than before. Yet, I wear them proudly!

As time passed, there were other encounters that threatened my survival as well as the sacred sites that had always been previously protected. One particular incident that threatened the ancient tar pit stands out in my memory. It came to my attention one day that this sacred site experienced a direct attack, and had it not been for my Interpreter friend from the museum, it may have been lost. He had removed a large quantity of trash that had been dumped into the asphalt springs over time and begun a preservation program to interpret the site for the public. By chance he was present one day when three self-propelled artillery vehicles roared into the area from the southwest and headed directly for the tar pit itself. He quickly ran to intercept them before they had trespassed too far into this historically sensitive area and caused irreparable damage with their churning metal tracks.

Positioning himself between the three armored vehicles and the tar pit site, he forced them to stop and tried desperately to wave them back toward the direction they had come from. The three vehicle commanders, wearing helmets and radio earphones, could not hear his shouts above the roaring engines. They were undoubtedly confused at his arm-waving antics and tried to go around him. Each time, however, he moved to block their path and continued waving them back. As they tried to move right, he blocked their path. When they tried to move left, he shifted accordingly.

Contemporary view toward the southwest of the Medicine Bluffs. The bluffs and their immediate environment are considered sacred ground by the local tribes and are listed on the National Register of Historic Places. (Photographer: Dedriech Swartz) (FSM)

The drivers raced their engines as an apparent warning for him to step aside, but he would not retreat. After some tense moments of confusion and stalemate, the three commanders finally turned their vehicles around and left the area. No doubt they were questioning what had just happened and may have considered this incident as an encounter with an unstable person on the east range that day. I was relieved that the problem had been averted and the tar pit site was spared.

As we enter the twenty-first century, I cannot help but worry about the future. Significant changes in the army's mission are causing greater impact on the buildings and landscape of Fort Sill, and it is becoming more crowded than ever before. I cannot help but recall a period of time after the cavalry left Fort Sill a little more than one hundred years ago in 1907 to 1909, when the army had to make some critical decisions about tearing down the old fort or relocating farther west to establish a new post for the artillery. It was a time of great turmoil, but fortunately, visionary people like President Theodore Roosevelt and Secretary of War William Howard Taft appreciated the history of Fort Sill and took a firm stand to preserve it for the future.

One hundred years later, that history is now being repeated. The army is once again faced with the same choices of preserving its history for future generations or destroying it to accommodate the requirements of a new mission. There is much conflict and confusion over this question, a fact that, I have often noticed in the past, brings out the best and sometimes the worst in people. It is times like this when people of vision, those who can see beyond the present circumstances, are desperately needed to protect the army's rich heritage for the future.

As a result of the Base Realignment and Closure Act (BRAC) in 2006, the Air Defense Artillery School was transferred from Fort Bliss, Texas, to Fort Sill and joined with the Field Artillery School to become the new "Fires Center of Excellence." The new logo depicts the joint mission of the two schools. (FSM)

Only a few of my kinsmen that were originally transplanted from the Medicine Bluffs Creek to the young fledgling fort in 1875 are still living today, and I am saddened by the loss of those that have not survived. A wandering raccoon climbed through my branches in the fall of 2008, spreading the alarm that one of the few original trees remaining from that event had been cut down in its prime.

The old hackberry tree that had been standing guard over the commander's quarters and the historic fort grounds for 134 years had fallen victim to uncaring people. They said it was a matter of safety, but they knew not of what they spoke. Although the foliage on its crown was becoming thinner with age, it was still healthy and fit for duty. Its only crime was getting older, but the army apparently mistrusted it and cut it down. What a shame! Where was the respect and appreciation for age and experience?

Beginning in 2007, even the sacred Medicine Bluffs were threatened with the construction of new buildings that would block its magnificent view and eliminate forever its access and use by the native people. But the warrior's pride resurfaced from the past, and the native people rose up in protest, threatening war over this sacred site. As my leaves began to fall in 2008, the Comanche Nation fought a great battle with the army in federal court, and once more, the survival of the old traditions was confronted with ignorance, poor judgment, and the perils of progress.

I witnessed many brave deeds during this conflict that reflected the spirit of the ancient past. During the trial, the tribal elders recounted the history from the old days in a desperate effort to enlighten their adversaries and prevent the destruction of this most sacred site. A Comanche warrior also relived his heritage in court by "counting coup" on his enemies with a "coup stick" as his ancestors had done on the battlefield more than 140 years before.

It was considered a very brave deed to get close enough to one's enemy and touch him with the coup stick rather than kill him from a distance. Several of the army witnesses waiting to testify in court were touched with the coup stick, and each heard the exclamation in the Comanche language, "I'm counting coup on you."

The same coup stick was used to protect my Interpreter friend from the scathing cross-examination by the U.S. Attorney during his testimony. It was discreetly placed in his lap under a black cloth while he sat in the witness chair enduring the hostile cross-examination. This relic from the past had been carried in combat by a native warrior/soldier during World War II.

The final day of the trial was held on the contested site at Fort Sill where both the light-colored people and the native people walked the sacred ground around the ancient bluffs in an effort to find a solution to this very serious problem.

As the judge deliberated his decision over the following days, I witnessed another old tradition from the past that was revived and carried out on the sacred ground south of the bluffs. A Comanche warrior who was descended from the Looking Glass family, dressed in his finest buckskin clothing complete with hair-pipe breastplate, fur turban, red and blue blankets, and eagle feathers, took position on the battlefield amidst the heavy construction equipment to await the judge's decision. He was later joined by another native warrior of the Chickasaw Nation—again my Interpreter friend from the museum—and both stood resolutely facing the bluffs armed with two traditional Comanche lances in uncertain expectation of what the future held for them.

The threatening earth scrapers, road graders, and bulldozers situated throughout the battlefield loomed menacingly over them like giant monsters, and the uncertainty of an enemy response kept them alert and prepared for anything. The falcons and hawks glided overhead toward the high bluffs, where they suddenly caught the rising air currents and soared upward before circling back to their starting point over the heads of the two warriors. These winged messengers of the sky then turned back toward the bluffs to repeat the cycle again.

I had witnessed this very traditional scene in the distant past when the highly committed warriors would pin themselves to the ground using a lance or stake while vowing not to leave the battlefield until they prevailed or until they were dead. After the battle, a surviving warrior could not leave the scene of combat until he was unpinned by another warrior. Fortunately, after much high drama and legal conflict, the native people prevailed in federal court, and the army changed its construction plans, leaving the Medicine Bluffs safe for the present.

Despite these very serious incidents, I continue to be hopeful that visionary leaders in the tradition of Presidents Roosevelt, Taft, and Truman will once again emerge on the scene and bring respect and reason to the destructive forces. They should not forget that the Medicine Bluffs, the ancient tar pit, and the historic trees were here long before the army came and obviously deserve its respect and protection. We witnessed the birth and development of Fort Sill, and the original stone buildings of the frontier post still survive today reminding everyone of the army's valiant struggles to accomplish its mission. We are as much a part of the army's rich heritage as the soldiers, their battles, and the equipment used in training and in combat all over the world. We are an important part of the cultural and physical homeland that the army has always defended, and it is only fitting that we should be protected accordingly.

During one mild winter day in 2010, an inspiring event occurred that I have seldom witnessed in my lifetime on Medicine Bluffs Creek. Following some brief evening showers and the equally brief emergence of the setting sun, a brilliantly colored rainbow appeared high in the eastern sky. The red, yellow, and blue colors were extremely vibrant and so much alive as to rival the most expansive fields of wildflowers one could imagine.

Not only were the colors unusually bright, but the steeply arcing curve of the rainbow brought both ends closer together than in a typical rainbow. The rainbow's northern end seemed to arc sharply downward, anchoring at the northeast corner of the historic fort grounds on the old stone chapel built in 1875. The opposing southern arc angled steeply to the ground near the southeast corner of the complex just behind the little wood frame building where the first headquarters for the School of Fire for Field Artillery was established in 1911.

This high arcing rainbow with its opposing ends so close together was unusual enough, but it was complemented by yet another separate rainbow just above it. This second or upper rainbow was more subdued than the lower one, but the bands of colors were still very bright and distinct.

The appearance and location of this phenomenal event seemed to signal a new beginning for saving the heritage of this most important place in time and space. Perhaps great leaders such as Roosevelt, Taft, and Truman have again emerged at Fort Sill, bringing renewed hope of protecting the historic landmarks, the sacred sites, and the natural beauty of this area from improper development in the future. Only time will tell!

Almost two-and-a-half centuries have passed since my original sprouting on the banks of Medicine Bluffs Creek, and I have witnessed many unusual dramas during that time. Although my deeply embedded roots have restricted any movement from this site, I have experienced a wondrous journey through time. In the process I have gained greater understanding and appreciation for all that has happened among the boulder-strewn slopes, dense oak forests, and grassy meadows of the Wichita Mountains. Still, the mystery of the future looms ahead of me. It is now more important than ever that I remain alert and continue serving as a "Silent Witness" to the history of Fort Sill.

Signed,
THE TREE

The author stands beside the Silent Witness tree after the devastating ice storm of January 28, 2010. (Photographer: Phyllis Spivey) (AUTH)

Epilogue: The Final Witness

Shortly after I completed this manuscript, a significant event occurred, beginning on the twenty-eighth day of January 2010, when a cataclysmic ice storm hit the Fort Sill area, leaving chaos and destruction in its wake. More than one hundred thousand people were left without electricity, heat, fuel, and communications in southwestern Oklahoma due to the plummeting temperatures, heavy ice, and cold north winds. The freedom of day-to-day activities involving working, living, and sleeping in a comfortable environment, traveling to and from any given destination, purchasing basic necessities, and otherwise enjoying the benefits of modern civilization, was totally disrupted.

On the morning of the second day after this epic event began, I went to the museum in the historic area of the post to assess the damage from the storm. Fort Sill was heavily impacted by this major weather phenomenon, and I was shocked at the carnage imposed on the trees. Passage on what had normally been passable roads and sidewalks was now made difficult by the debris scattered everywhere. Large limbs had fallen on the roofs of the historic buildings, and normal access to entrances was impossible in many places. The entire area looked like a bomb had exploded over the landscape. Not a single tree was spared from split trunks, broken limbs, or complete collapse. I noted with dismay that two of the last four historic trees planted by Colonel Ranald Mackenzie at the close of the Red River War in 1875 had fallen victim to this vicious storm. The landscape was almost unrecognizable!

It was with a sense of reluctance and foreboding that I traveled the short distance to the golf course and the wooded area along Medicine Bluffs Creek to check on the Silent Witness tree as I had done countless times over the years. It was impossible to drive directly to the immediate area of the tree because of the many fallen tree trunks and limbs across the terrain, so it was necessary to walk the last quarter-mile. The absence of tracks in the snow indicated that no one else had been to this area since the onset of the storm. Drawing near the site of the tree, I was hesitant to look up from the tangled masses of snow-covered limbs and debris on the ground.

Slowly raising my head, I could not avoid the stark image of the large naked trunk projecting upward and still towering defiantly over the other trees in the area. Unfortunately, the ancient oak had been decapitated and also dismembered of all limbs, leaving it looking very much like a huge, jagged fence post. The original crown of the tree stood inverted beside the trunk, and virtually all of the large limbs lay on the surrounding forest floor radiating outward from the trunk like the spokes of a giant wheel. The tree had not survived the harsh winter ice storm.

It was a scene reminiscent of the destruction left in some of the great cities of England, other European countries, and Japan after the massive aerial bombings during World War II. In this case, however, the destruction was the result of an act of God. While I stared at the tree, the deafening silence of the forest was sporadically interrupted by loud cracking noises from the large limbs on nearby trees, straining under their burden of heavy ice before finally crashing perilously to the ground as though to punctuate the final moments of life for the ancient oak tree.

There was a sense of tragedy that after approximately 250 years the journey of this giant bur oak tree had come to an end. The final act of this magnificent tree was to witness a most historic ice storm that wreaked havoc on both the people and the landscape of southwestern Oklahoma. Only six days before, there had been an unusual double rainbow in the skies over Fort Sill that seemed to prophesize the coming of a major event, much the same as the meteorite shower had done for the Kiowa people in 1833. As with the Kiowa, however, there was no way to predict the exact nature of that event or what the result would be.

After a tragedy such as this, we are left with certain basic questions that reflect our appreciation, or lack thereof, for the history and traditions of the world around us. When experiencing relationships between people of different cultural traditions and values, during conflict and tragedy, success and failure, can we also find common ground for respect and mutual understanding? Can we come to terms with the fact that we must also protect and share our space with the historic monuments that remind us of the struggles, the accomplishments, the successes, and the failures from the past? For without these monuments, there are no guideposts to the future. It has been said that when a nation has lost its past, it has also lost its future!

Is this the legacy of the Silent Witness tree? Are there other ancient trees or living monuments yet to be discovered that might also serve as witnesses to our history? If so, where are the Interpreters who could understand and speak for them, and more importantly, would anyone listen? Can we learn from the lessons of our history and appreciate the world around us from the perspective of a tree? The answers to these questions remain uncertain and must be left for each of us to ponder in our own way and in our own time.

Signed,
TOWANA SPIVEY
THE INTERPRETER

Selected References

Brash, Sarah, ed. *The American Story—Defiant Chiefs, 1810-1910.* Alexandria, VA: Time-Life Books, 1997.

Collinwood, G. H., and Warren D. Brush. (Revised and edited by Bevereux Butcher.) *Know Your Trees.* Washington, DC: The American Forestry Association, 1978.

Florin, Lambert. *Historic Glimpses of Trees in the West: A Journey with Lambert Florin.* Seattle, WA: Superior Publishing Company, 1977.

Hagan, William T. *Quanah Parker, Comanche Chief.* Norman: University of Oklahoma, 1993.

Haislet, John A., ed. *Famous Trees of Texas.* Austin: Texas Forest Service, 1970.

Holling, Holling Clancy. *Tree in the Trail.* Boston: Houghton Mifflin Company, 1970.

Leckie, William H. *The Buffalo Soldiers: A Narrative of the Negro Cavalry in the West.* Norman: University of Oklahoma, 1967.

Meadows, William C. *The Comanche Code Talkers of World War II.* Austin: University of Texas Press, 2002.

Michno, Gregory F. *Encyclopedia of Indian Wars: Western Battles and Skirmishes, 1850–1890.* Missoula, MT: Mountain Press Publishing Company, 2003.

Neeley, Bill. *The Last Comanche Chief: The Life and Times of Quanah Parker.* New York: John Wiley & Sons, Inc., 1995.

Nye, Col Wilbur S. *Carbine and Lance: The Story of Old Fort Sill.* Norman: University of Oklahoma, 1935, revised edition of 1974.

Nye, Wilbur Sturtevant. *Plains Indian Raiders.* Norman: University of Oklahoma Press, 1968.

Selected References cont.

Prose, Maryruth, and Towana Spivey. *Bison: From the Prehistoric Past to the American Frontier.* Duncan, OK: The Cross Timbers Press, 1983.

Shirley, Glenn. *West of Hell's Fringe.* Norman: University of Oklahoma Press, 1978.

Smith, Thomas T., ed. *A Dose of Frontier Soldiering, The Memoirs of Corporal E. A. Bode, Frontier Regular Infantry, 1877–1882.* Lincoln: University of Nebraska Press, 1994.

Spivey, Towana. "Early Base Ball at Fort Sill." Fort Sill, OK: Fort Sill National Historic Landmark Museum, 2007.

———. "Notes from an Interview with MG Hugh Franklin Foster, WWII Training Officer for the Comanche Code Talkers—16 May 1991." Fort Sill, OK: Fort Sill National Historic Landmark Museum, 1991.

———. "Pass in Review—A History of Fort Sill." Fort Sill, OK: Fort Sill National Historic Landmark Museum, 2009.

———. "Personal Interviews with Ernst Schriewer, Josef Euteneuer, Karl Kurth, et al., Former German POWs at Fort Sill," Fort Sill, OK: Fort Sill National Historic Landmark Museum, 1992–2004.

———. "Personal Interviews with Forest Kassanavoid and Charles Chibitty, Comanche Code Talkers," Fort Sill, OK: Fort Sill National Historic Landmark Museum,1995–2003.

———. "Personal Interview with Lieutenant Ernest Childers, WWII Medal of Honor Recipient," Fort Sill, OK: Fort Sill National Historic Landmark Museum, 1989.

———. "Personal Interviews with Mildred Cleghorn and Benedict Johze, Former Apache POWs at Fort Sill," Fort Sill, OK: Fort Sill National Historic Landmark Museum, 1985–1994.

————. "Silent Witness" in *Prairie Lore.* Lawton, OK: Southwestern Oklahoma Historical Society, Vol. 33, No. 1, Book No. 98, Spring, 1997.

————. "Silent Witness" in *The Fort Sill Dispatch,* A Publication of the Fort Sill Museum, Fort Sill, OK: June/July/August, 1999.

————. "Troop L, Seventh Cavalry" in *The Fort Sill Dispatch,* A Publication of the Fort Sill Museum, Fort Sill, OK: Issue #2, 2000.

————. "Warriors in Blue: The Indian Soldiers of Troop L, 7th US Cavalry, Fort Sill, Oklahoma Territory." Fort Sill, OK: Fort Sill National Historic Landmark Museum, 2003.

————. "You Are There—The Incident at Sherman House, Fort Sill, Indian Territory, 27 May 1871." Fort Sill, OK: Fort Sill National Historic Landmark Museum, 2008.

Spivey, Towana, et al. *Archeological Investigations Along the Waurika Pipeline.* Lawton, OK: Museum of the Great Plains, 1975.

Swett, Morris. "The Splendid Pageant" in *The Fort Sill Dispatch,* A Publication of the Fort Sill Museum, Fort Sill, OK: November/December/January 1999/2000 (extracted from "Fort Sill: A History," 1921).

Utley, Robert M. *Cavalier in Buckskin, George Armstrong Custer and the Western Military Frontier.* Norman: University of Oklahoma Press, 1988.

Wright, Muriel A. *A Guide to the Indian Tribes of Oklahoma.* Norman: University of Oklahoma Press, 1986.

About the Author

As a historian, archeologist, and museum curator with many years experience in the southern plains region, Towana Spivey has authored numerous historical publications and participated in television documentaries throughout the world. He has also lectured on military and frontier history as well as Native American culture. Spivey is a member of the Chickasaw Nation, with ancestors who immigrated to the Indian Territory in 1837 and who also participated in the 1858 expedition to the Medicine Bluffs area.

In 1984, the prophetic name "The Last One Standing at Sunrise" was bestowed on the author by George "Woogie" Watchetaker, world champion war dancer, prominent artist, traditional medicine man, and brother of Comanche code-talker Charles Chibitty.

Spivey's narratives regarding the history of southwest Oklahoma and the western frontier were recorded by the *Voice of America* for broadcasting behind the Iron Curtain of the Soviet Union shortly before the Berlin Wall came down in 1989. He has served for many years as the director and curator of the Fort Sill National Historic Landmark Museum at Fort Sill, Oklahoma.